WASHOKU

Japanese Traditional Food and Food Culture

松本美江〔著〕
MATSUMOTO Yoshie〔Author〕

JN112028

ブックデザイン	池田香奈子
イラスト	福岡麻利子
英文チェック	久松紀子
英文校正	フレヤ・マーティン
編集協力	吉原朋江（株式会社スリーシーズン）
編集担当	横山美穂（ナツメ出版企画株式会社）

Author   MATSUMOTO Yoshie

BA in English Literature from Doshisha University. MA in Linguistics and TESOL from the University of Colorado at Boulder, USA.
Since passing the national licensed interpreter-guide examination, Yoshie Matsumoto has guided thousands of tourists from all over the world for over 30 years. She is the chairman of the Japan Federation of Certified Guides (JFG), and she is also in charge of training for those who have passed the national interpreter-guide exam. Her books include "All About Japan-A Bilingual Handbook for Visitors and Interpreter-Guides" (Japan Times Publishing), "Experience Japan" (Natsumesha), and "An Introductory Handbook to Japan and its People" (ALC).

Book Design	IKEDA Kanako
Illustration	FUKUOKA Mariko
English Checker	HISAMATSU Noriko
English Proofreader	Freya Martin
Associate Editor	YOSHIHARA Tomoe (Three season Co.,Ltd.)
Editor	YOKOYAMA Miho (Natsume Shuppan Kikaku Co.,Ltd.)

WASHOKU
Japanese Traditional Food and Food Culture
First Edition June 2021

Publisher
Natsumesha Co.,Ltd.
Natsume Bldg. 1F 1-52 Kanda -Jimbocho, Chiyoda-ku, Tokyo, Japan 101-0051

Production
Natsume Shuppan Kikaku Co., Ltd.

Printing
Lan Printing Co.,Ltd

目次
Contents

コ ラ ム
Column

Part **1**

寿司／刺身
Sushi / Sashimi

寿司は人気の高い和食です。マグロのセリは、事前予約をすると豊洲で見学できます。

Sushi is a very popular food. You can watch the tuna auction in Toyosu by making a reservation.

にぎり寿司
Nigiri-zushi

細巻
Hosomaki (Thin *Sushi* Roll)

太巻
Hutomaki (Thick *Sushi* Roll)

手巻き寿司
Hand-rolled *Sushi*

ちらし寿司
Chirashi-zushi

刺身
Sashimi

フグ刺し
Puffer Fish *Sashimi*

カツオのタタキ
Bonito *Sashimi Tataki*-style

マグロのやまかけ
Tuna *Yamakake*-style

アジのなめろう
Aji (Horse Mackerel) *Namero*-style

にぎり寿司

[Nigiri-zushi]

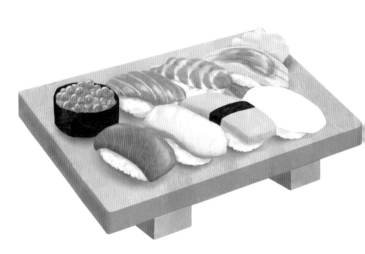

手のひらの上で形を整えたごはんに、
生の魚介類などをのせたものです。
**Toppings of raw fish and seafood on rice shaped in the
palm of the hand.**

寿司用のごはんを「シャリ」、その上にのせる食材を「ネ
タ」とよびます。シャリは、酢と調味料を混ぜ合わせて、
冷ましたごはん（すし飯）です。ネタの種類はさまざまで、
生の魚介類がメインです。甘い卵焼きも伝統的なネタ
です。
寿司屋で食べるときには、好きなネタを選んでにぎって
もらうか、セットを注文します。カウンターに座ると、板
前さんが、あっという間に寿司をにぎってくれますが、そ
うした職人技を眺められるのも、楽しみのひとつです。

The rice base for *sushi (zushi)* is called "*shari*," and
the ingredients placed on it are called "*neta*." *Shari* is
prepared by cooling the rice after it mixing in some
vinegar and seasonings. There are various types
of *neta*, but they are mainly different kinds of raw
seafood. Sweet omelet is also a traditional *neta*.
When you eat at a *sushi* bar, you can order your choice
of *neta* or a set menu. One of the pleasures of sitting
at the counter is that you can see the *sushi* chef's
craftsmanship in making hand-rolled *sushi* in no time.

寿司のネタいろいろ

[Types of *Neta*]

マグロ （大トロ・中トロ・赤身）
Tuna (high-fat tuna, medium fatty tuna, red meat)

マグロには獲れる場所によって、さまざまな種類がありますが、「本マグロ」とよばれる、太平洋クロマグロと大西洋クロマグロが人気です。

There are various types of tuna depending on where they are caught. However Pacific bluefin tuna and Atlantic bluefin tuna, which are called "real tuna," are popular.

マグロの部位
Parts of the Tuna

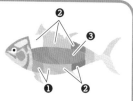

マグロ一頭から約1万個のにぎり寿司ができるといわれています。マグロの部位によって、ネタとしてのよび方が変わります。

It is said that about 10,000 *nigiri-zushi* can be made from one tuna. Depending on the part of the tuna used for the topping, the *sushi neta* made from tuna are called by different names.

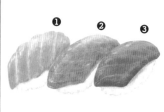

❶ 「大トロ」は、脂肪分がとても多い部分です。
❶ "*Oh Toro*" contains a lot of fat.

❷ 「中トロ」は、筋肉質と脂肪分を合わせもっています。
❷ "*Chu Toro*" has both muscle and fat content.

❸ 「赤身」は、脂肪分が少ない筋肉質の部分です。
❸ "*Akami*" has high muscle content and a small amount of fat.

サーモン
Salmon

ほどよい脂の甘味があります。
人気のネタです。

Salmon has an adequate
amount of fat and sweetness.
It is a popular *sushi* topping.

イカ
Squid

新鮮な生のイカは白く透き通っ
ています。甘味が魅力です。

Fresh squid is white and
transparent. Its sweet taste is
appealing.

タコ
Octopus

ゆでてスライスしてネタにするの
が一般的です。

Octopus is usually used as a
topping after it has been boiled
and sliced.

寿司のネタいろいろ

[Types of *Neta*]

エビ
Shrimp

生で食べるものと、ゆでて食べるものがあります。

Some shrimp *neta* are served raw whereas others are boiled.

ウニ
Sea urchin

高級な寿司ネタです。旨みと甘みがたっぷりで人気があります。

An expensive topping, the sea urchin is popular because it has full of *umami* (fifth category of taste) and sweetness.

イクラ
Salmon roe

シャリを海苔で巻いて、その上にイクラをのせます（軍艦巻きといいます）。

Salmon roe is usually placed on top of a *sushi* rice roll that has an outer wrapping of *nori*.

ホタテ
Scallop

北国の浅瀬に生息する貝です。
強い甘味と旨みがあります。
The scallop is a type of shellfish
that lives in the shallow waters of
northern Japan.
It has strong sweetness and
umami.

ホヤ
Sea squirt

パイナップルのような形の貝で
す。魚市場でぜひ見てください。
You can see these sea squirts
that are shaped like a pineapple
at the fish market.

ミル貝
***Mirugai* clams**

独特な形を魚市場で見てくださ
い。甘味と旨みが特徴です。
You can see the unique shape
of these clams at the fish
market. They are known for
their sweetness and *umami.*

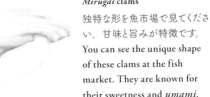

細巻

[*Hosomaki* (Thin *Sushi* Roll)]

のりとすし飯の上にネタをおき、細く巻いた寿司です。
Hosomaki is a type of *sushi* in the shape of a thin roll
that contains *sushi* rice and one other ingredients inside
an outer layer of *nori*.

「巻きす」という竹でできた道具を使ってつくります。細切りのきゅ
うりを入れたものは「かっぱ巻き」、マグロの赤身を入れたもの
は「鉄火巻き」、マグロの中落ちという部位とねぎを細かくたた
いたものは「ねぎトロ巻き」とよびます。
A bamboo mat called a "*makisu*" is used to roll the rice and
ingredients inside the *nori* wrapping. The *hosomaki* that
contains shredded cucumber is called a "*kappa* roll," the one
made using lean tuna is called a "*tekka* roll," and the one that
is made with chopped tuna meat from the spine of the fish
and green onion is called a "*negitoro* roll."

太巻

[*Hutomaki* (Thick *Sushi* Roll)]

のりとすし飯の上にたくさんのネタをおき、巻きすで太く巻いた寿司です。

Hutomaki is a thick sushi roll that contains *sushi* rice and a lot of ingredients wrapped inside *nori* with a *makisu*.

太巻は細巻きよりも、多くのネタを入れてつくります。だし巻き卵、しいたけやかんぴょうの煮物、きゅうり、エビなどを巻きます。節分の夜に、その年の恵方（縁起の良い方角）を向いて太巻を丸かじりすると、福が来るといわれています。

Thick rolls can hold more ingredients than thin rolls, including *dashimaki* omelet, simmered *shiitake* mushrooms, *kanpyo*, cucumbers and shrimps. It is said that fortune comes when facing the *eho* (the auspicious direction) of the year and eating a whole thick roll without cutting it on the night of *setsubun* (the day before the beginning of spring).

手巻き寿司

[Hand-rolled *Sushi*]

好みの具を入れて、家庭で手軽につくれる寿司です。
You can easily make hand-rolled *sushi* at home using
your favorite ingredients.

手巻き寿司は、家庭料理としても人気があります。海苔、すし飯、好きなネタを用意するだけでつくることができるので簡単です。手軽に準備のできる、キュウリやツナは子どもにも人気です。また、通常は寿司屋でネタにされることはありませんが、照り焼きチキンや焼き肉やレタスなどを入れてもおいしく食べられます。寿司屋でも、巻き物のメニューで細巻きか手巻きを選べるところがあります。

Hand-rolled *sushi* is also popular as a home-made dish. Making hand-rolled *sushi* is simple because you can make it just by preparing *nori*, *sushi* rice and your favorite ingredients. Cucumbers and tuna, which are easy to prepare, are also popular with children. Unusual *sushi* ingredients, such as *teriyaki* chicken, grilled meat and lettuce are delicious too. At some *sushi* bars, you can often choose between thin *sushi* rolls made using a *makisu* and hand-rolled *sushi*.

ちらし寿司

[*Chirashi-zushi*]

すし飯に色とりどりのネタや具をのせたものです。
Sushi rice topped with colorful ingredients.

すし飯を四角や丸い形の塗器などに入れて、その上に
ネタ、錦糸卵（細切りにした卵焼き）、しいたけやかんぴょ
うの煮物、おぼろ（白身魚やエビをすりつぶし、味付
けして煮たもの）、しょうがなどをちらすようにのせたもの
です。東京以外の地域では、ネタはのせないこともあり
ます。見た目が華やかなので、お祝いの日などに家庭
でつくることもあります。

Chirashi-zushi is served in a square or round lacquered
lunch box. Various kinds of ingredients such as
seafood, shredded thin omelet, simmered *kanpyo*,
shiitake mashrooms, *oboro* (mashed and seasoned white
fish and shrimps) and red pickled ginger are scattered
on top of *sushi* rice. In areas other than Tokyo, this
type of *sushi* is often served without seafood. As it
looks so gorgeous, it is sometimes prepared at home on
celebration days.

寿司のはじまり

Origin of *sushi*

寿司の元祖は「なれずし」と言って、塩漬けにした魚
とご飯を乳酸発酵させたものでした。当時はごはんは
食べずに捨てていました。今から800年ほど前に、魚
とご飯を一緒に食べる現在の箱寿司のようになったそう
です。

The origin of *sushi* was *nare-zushi*, salted fish and rice
fermented by lactic acid. The rice was not eaten but
thrown away. From about 800 years ago, people started
to eat both fish and rice packed in a box, which is like
today's *Hako-zushi* (Boxed *sushi*).

箱寿司
Hako-zushi (Boxed *sushi*)

四角の木製の箱に、すし飯
とネタをのせて押しかためて
作る寿司。
Sushi made by putting
sushi rice and ingredients
in a square wooden box and
pressing them.

今のにぎり寿司のようになったのは江戸時代（1603 ～ 1867 年）です。江戸湾で獲れた魚介類を、今より大きなすし飯の上にのせ、屋台の食事として人気になりました。

It was in the Edo period (1603-1867) that *nigiri-zushi* much larger than *sushi* balls today topped with sea food caught in Edo Bay were served at mobile stalls and became popular.

刺身

[*Sashimi*]

新鮮な魚介類の切り身を生で食べます。
Sashimi are slices of fresh fish and seafood that are served raw.

さばいて一口サイズにした新鮮な魚介類の切り身に、
しょうゆやわさびをつけて食べます。
寿司屋や居酒屋で「盛り合わせ」を注文すると、通
常マグロや白身の魚、季節の魚を選んで一皿に盛り合
わせてくれます。魚のほかに、海老、イカ、貝類、ウ
ニなどが追加されることもあります。刺身の盛り合わせは、
宴会料理として、とても人気があります。

You can eat fresh fish and seafood that have been sliced
into bite-sized pieces with soy sauce and *wasabi*.
When you order "assorted *sashimi*" at a *sushi* bar or
izakaya, usually tuna, white fish, and seasonal fish
selected for you are served on one plate. Sometimes,
shrimps, squids, shellfish, sea urchin may also be
added to the assortment of fish. Assorted *sashimi* is
also very popular as a banquet dish.

フグ刺し

[Puffer Fish *Sashimi*]

淡白ながら旨みの詰まったフグの刺身は高級品です。
Puffer fish *sashimi* tastes bland but is full of *umami* and
is a luxury item.

猛毒があることで知られており、誰がその毒にあたるか分からな
いという意味をこめて「ロシアン・ルーレット」とよぶ人もいますが、
日本では、専門の調理免許を持った料理人がさばきます。皿
の模様が見えるほど薄くスライスされて出されます。
Some people describe the eating of this *sashimi* as "Russian
roulette" because the fish is known to be highly poisonous and
you do not know whether you could get poisoned. In Japan,
only chefs with a specialized cooking license are allowed to
clean and cut puffer fish. It is served sliced so thinly that the
pattern on the serving plate can be seen through it.

カツオのタタキ

[Bonito *Sashimi Tataki*-style]

表面だけ焼いた、カツオの刺身です。
Bonito *sashimi* grilled only on the surface.

カツオの切り身の表面だけ火を入れ、中は生の状態にしたもの
を、冷やしてスライスします。伝統的な焼き方では、乾燥した
藁などに火をつけて焼きます。ポン酢に刻みねぎ、おろししょうが、
にんにくの薄切りなどを加えて食べます。

Tataki-style bonito is grilled only its surface, so it remains
raw inside. After it has been cooled, it is sliced and served.
Traditionally, it is grilled by placing it over ignited dried
straw. It is recommended that you eat it by dipping it in *ponzu*
sauce together with chopped spring onion, grated ginger and
thin garlic slices.

25

マグロのやまかけ

[Tuna *Yamakake*-style]

ヤマイモのすりおろしをかけた、マグロの赤身の刺身です。
Red tuna *sashimi* topped with grated *yamaimo* yam.

しょうゆ、みりん、わさびのタレで下味をつけたマグロの刺身に、
「とろろ」とよばれるヤマイモのすりおろしをかけたものです。と
ろろのネバネバした食感はめずらしく、海外の方には、はじめ
て食べるという方も多くいます。

Grated *yamaimo* yam called "*tororo*" is placed on top of tuna
that has been marinated in soy sauce, *mirin* and *wasabi*. For
many foreign visitors, this sticky texture is a new experience
to try.

アジのなめろう

[*Aji* (Horse Mackerel) *Namero*-style]

アジの刺身を細かくたたき、味付けしたものです。
Horse mackerel *sashimi* finely chopped and seasoned.

アジの刺身を、しょうゆ、みそ、おろしにんにく、おろししょうが、ねぎなどと一緒に、包丁でたたいて混ぜたものです。居酒屋で人気が高く、ビールや日本酒などのお酒のおつまみに合います。

Horse mackerel *sashimi* is chopped and mixed together with grated garlic, grated ginger, spring onion, *miso*, and soy sauce. It is very popular in *izakaya* as a type of nibbles for *sake* and beer.

27

日本の各地の美味しい魚介類

Tasty seafood in various parts of Japan

大間のマグロ
Tuna in Oma

北海道と本州の間の津軽海峡にはプランクトンを豊富に含んだ海流が流れこむことから、イカやイワシが集まってきます。青森県大間町は、そのイカやイワシをエサに大きく育ったクロマグロの一本釣りが盛んです。これが、「大間のマグロ」として知られています。新年恒例のマグロの初セリでは、大間ブランドのクロマグロが例年驚くほどの価格で競り落とされますが、その光景が全国ニュースになっています。

The Tsugaru Strait between Hokkaido and Honshu is where squids and sardines are attracted by the rich plankton contained in the flowing ocean current. Oma port is known for the pole-and-line fishing of tuna which grow big eating the squids and sardines. Every year we hear the news reporting that Oma brand bluefin tuna has been fetched at an amazingly high price at the New Year auction of tuna.

広島の牡蠣
Oysters in Hiroshima

広島県は、牡蠣養殖生産量が日本一で、全生産量の半数を占めています。世界遺産の宮島へ就航するフェリーからも養殖筏が見えるため、海外の方からも関心を集めています。広島湾は波が小さく、多くの川が流れ込み、豊富なプランクトンが集まるので牡蠣の養殖に適しているそうです。

Hiroshima prefecture produces the highest proportion of cultured oysters in Japan, amounting to 50% of national production. Foreign visitors are amazed to see the oyster rafts as they approach Miyajima, a World Heritage site, by ferry. It is said that Hiroshima Bay is suitable for oyster culture because plankton gather in the bay where the waves are calm and many rivers flow into it.

Part 2

丼ぶり／米
Donburi / Rice

米は日本の主食です。日本では 3000 年以上も前から稲が育てられてきました。
Rice is a Japanese staple food. Rice has been cultivated in Japan for about 3000 years.

32/

牛丼
Gyu-don (Beef Bowl)

34/

親子丼
Oyako-don (Parent and Child Bowl)

36/

かつ丼
Katsu-don

37/

天丼
Ten-don

38/

海鮮丼
Kaisen-don

39/

うな重（うな丼）
Unaju (Una-don)

42/

おにぎり / おむすび
Onigiri / Omusubi
(Flavored-rice Balls)

44/

炊き込みごはん
Takikomi Gohan

46/

赤飯
Sekihan
(Rice Cooked with Red Beans)

47/

茶漬け
Chazuke

48/

雑炊
Zosui (Rice Porridge)

50/

カレーライス
Curry and Rice

52/

オムライス
Omurice

54/

ハヤシライス
Hayashi Rice

56-57/

磯部焼き
Isobe Yaki

きなこもち
Kinako Mochi

牛丼

[*Gyu-don* (Beef Bowl)]

牛肉と玉ねぎの甘辛煮をのせた丼です。

A bowl of rice topped with sweet and salty beef and onions.

丼ぶりに入れたごはんの上に、さまざまな具をのせたも
のを「丼」とよび、具の種類によって名前が変わります。
「牛丼」は、牛肉の薄切りと玉ねぎをしょうゆやみりん
で煮たものをのせたものです。「温泉卵」とよばれる半
熟の卵や、紅しょうがをのせることもあります。日本の牛
丼チェーン店は 1975 年から海外進出しており、海外
では Beef Bowl として知っている方も多くいます。

A bowl of rice topped with various ingredients is
called a "*don*," and the name changes depending on
the toppings. So, "*gyu-don*" is rice topped with sliced
beef (*gyu*) and onions simmered in soy sauce and
mirin. A soft-boiled egg called "*onsen tamago*" or red
pickled ginger may also be placed on top. Japanese beef
bowl chain restaurants have been expanding in other
countries since 1975, and many people overseas know
this dish as beef bowl.

親子丼

[*Oyako-don* (Parent and Child Bowl)]

ふわとろな卵、鶏肉と玉ねぎの煮物をのせた丼です。
A bowl of rice topped with fluffy eggs, simmered
chicken and onions.

鶏肉が親、卵が子どもと、材料が親子なので「親子丼」
とよびます。おいしくて体にやさしい人気の丼です。一
口大にした鶏肉とスライスした玉ねぎを、しょうゆ、砂糖
（または、みりん）、だしで煮たものに、溶き卵をまわし
かけ、ごはんにのせたものです。三つ葉を刻んだものを
のせて、香りと彩りがプラスされます。

The bowl is named "*oyako-don*" because the
ingredients, namely chicken and egg, are the parent
and the child, respectively.

Oyako-don is a popular bowl of food that is delicious
and gentle on the body. It is prepared by simmering
bite-sized chicken and sliced onions in soy sauce,
sugar (or *mirin*), and *dashi* stock over which beaten
eggs are poured and simmered a little. This topping is
then placed on the rice. Scent and color are added by
putting chopped trefoil on it.

かつ丼

[*Katsu-don*]

ボリュームたっぷりのとんかつをのせた丼です。

A substantial bowl of rice topped with pork cutlet.

食べやすい大きさに切ったとんかつと玉ねぎを、しょうゆ、砂糖
（または、みりん）、だしで煮て、溶き卵をまわしかけ、あつあ
つのごはんにのせたものです。千切りキャベツの上にとんかつ
のせて、とんかつソースをかける「ソースかつ丼」もあります。

This bowl is prepared by slicing pork cutlet into finger-sized
length, simmering it and onions in soy sauce, sugar (or *mirin*),
and *dashi* broth. And then beaten eggs are poured over it.
These ingredients are then placed on hot rice. Another type of
"*katsu-don*" is the "sauce *katsu-don*." This rice bowl is made
by placing the pork cutlet on shredded cabbage and pouring
tonkatsu sauce on top.

天丼

[*Ten-don*]

天つゆで味つけした天ぷらをのせた丼です。
**Hot rice topped with freshly fried *tempura* dipped in
sweet soy-based sauce.**

天ぷらを甘辛い天つゆにさっと通し、あつあつのごはんの上に
のせたものです。とくに人気があるのは、大きめの海老の天ぷ
らがのっているものです。天ぷら屋のほか、そば屋でも人気の
あるメニューです。手軽に天ぷらを楽しむことができます。
Hot rice is topped with freshly fried *tempura* dipped in
"*tentsuyu*," which literally means "dip sauce for *tempura*." The
most popular *ten-don* is the one with large prawn *tempura*. It
is a popular menu item not only in *tempura* restaurants but
also in *soba* restaurants. *Soba* restaurants are the easy places
for you to enjoy *tempura*.

海鮮丼

[*Kaisen-don*]

さまざまな種類の海鮮の刺身がのった丼です。
A bowl of rice topped with various kinds of *sashimi* and seafood.

海鮮丼は、ごはんの上に海鮮の刺身をたっぷりのせたものです。マグロの刺身、サーモン、イクラ、エビ、カニ、イカ、ホタテが人気のネタです。わさびを溶いたしょうゆをかけて食べます。ちらし寿司と似ていますが、すし飯ではありません。
Tuna, salmon, salmon roe, shrimps, crabs, squids and scallops are popular ingredients for *kaisen-don*. Eat this dish by sprinkling soy sauce with *wasabi* on it. The ingredients are similar to *chirashi-zushi*, but *sushi* rice is not used.

うな重（うな丼）

[*Unaju (Una-don)*]

四角いお重にごはんを入れ、うなぎのかば焼きをのせたものです。

Unagi (eel) *kabayaki* is placed on top of rice served in a square lacquered box.

お重に入れたら「うな重」、丼ぶりに入れたら「うな丼」とよびます。日本では、うなぎは精をつける食べ物で、夏バテ防止にきくといわれ、体力が落ちる夏に食べる習慣があります。近年、稚魚が減ってしまって価格が高騰し、贅沢なものになっています。

This dish is called "*Unaju*" when served in a box and "*Unadon*" when served in a bowl. In Japan, eel is believed to increase one's vitality and prevent heat fatigue. In Japan, the summer is terribly hot and humid, so it is customary to eat it during this season when physical strength is low. The number of young eels has decreased in recent years, and so their price has soared, making this dish a luxury item.

ごはんを鍋で炊く方法

How to cook rice in a pot

ごはんは、炊飯器でもおいしく炊けますが、鍋で炊く方法を紹介します。米を手早く洗い、水がきれいになるまで繰り返します。洗った米にその 1.1〜1.2 倍の水を足し、20 分くらい置いておくのがおいしく炊くためのコツです。加熱して最初は強火、沸騰したら弱火にして 10 分くらい火にかけます。炊きあがってもすぐに蓋を取らず、10 分くらい蒸すと出来上がりです。

Rice can be cooked deliciously using a rice cooker, but here is how to cook it in a pot. First, wash the rice quickly by changing the water until the water becomes clear. The secret of success is to then soak the rice in an amount of water 1.1 to 1.2 times the amount of rice, for about 20 minutes. Place the pan on a high heat and bring it to the boil. Then lower the heat and simmer for about 10 minutes. Do not open the lid immediately after it is done. Instead, let cooked rice sit after turning off the heat for 10 minutes. Then it is ready.

おにぎりのにぎり方

How to make *Onigiri*

1. 手をきれいに洗ってから手のひらに塩を
ふります。片手にごはんをのせて、好みの
具を真ん中に置きます。具をくるむようにご
はんを丸めましょう。

1. Sprinkle salt on your clean hands, put
rice in one hand, and put your favorite
ingredients in the middle. Then roll
the rice so that it wraps around the
ingredients.

2. 両手で三角を作るように形づくります。
手の角度とごはんの位置を変えて数回にぎ
ります。ごはんの粒を押しつぶさず、中は
ふんわりさせます。

2. Hold it with both hands to shape it
into a triangle. Grip it several times by
changing the angle of your hands and the
position of the rice. Do not press it too
hard, but make the inside fluffy.

3. 最後にパリッとした焼き海苔でくるみます。
3. Finally, wrap it in crispy grilled *nori*
kelp.

おにぎり / おむすび

[*Onigiri / Omusubi* (Flavored-rice Balls)]

炊き立てのごはんに具を入れ、三角ににぎったものです。
**Made by adding various ingredients to freshly cooked
rice and shaping by hand into a triangular shape.**

ごはんに入れる具はさまざまです。中に具を入れるだけではな
く、具を混ぜたごはんや、炊き込みごはんでつくることもあります。
持ち運びに便利な携帯食なので、日本版のサンドイッチともい
えます。学校行事の運動会や遠足に持っていくことが多く、子
どものころの楽しい思い出につながります。

When making *onigiri*, a range of ingredients is added to the
rice. In addition to putting ingredients in the middle of the
rice ball, sometimes the cooked rice is mixed with the other
ingredients or the rice is cooked with the chosen ingredients
at the same time. The *onigiri* is said to be the Japanese
version of the sandwich because it is a handy, portable food.
Children often take them to sports events and on school field
trips, which makes them a part of their happy memories of
childhood.

具のいろいろ

[Types of *Onigiri* / *Omusubi*]

梅干し
Umeboshi → P154参照 see page 154

抗菌作用もあり、すっぱさが食欲をそそる定番の具です。

A classic ingredient, *umeboshi*, is a type of plum with an antibacterial effect, and its sourness is appetizing.

焼きザケ
Grilled salmon

焼きザケの身を切ったり、ほぐしたりしていれます。

You can cut or flake grilled salmon for use as a topping.

小エビの天ぷら
Small shrimp *tempura*

天ぷらおむすびを略して、「天むす」とよびます。名古屋の名物で知られています。

Omusubi with a small-shrimp *tempura* is called "*tenmusu*," which is a shortened version of the name "*tempura* and *omusubi* (*onigiri*)." It is known as a specialty of Nagoya.

炊き込みごはん

[*Takikomi Gohan*]

米と具を入れて、だしで炊いたごはんです。
Rice cooked with *dashi* broth and ingredients.

具と一緒に炊くごはんを「炊き込みごはん」といいます。具は
さまざまですが、鶏肉、たけのこ、にんじん、きのこ、油揚げなど、
5種類の具を入れた「五目ごはん」は定番です。季節を感じ
る旬の食材を入れることも多いです。
Rice cooked with ingredients is called "*takikomi gohan*."
Various ingredients can be used, but "*gomoku gohan*,"
which means rice with five kinds of ingredients is standard.
Traditionally, the five ingredients are chicken, bamboo shoots,
carrots, mushrooms, and fried *tofu*. However, often seasonal
ingredients are used.

具のいろいろ

[Types of *Takikomi Gohan*]

たけのこごはん
Takenoko gohan

春が旬のたけのこを入れて炊き込みます。食感を楽しみます。
Rice cooked with bamboo shoots, a seasonal ingredient in springtime. This is the perfect time to enjoy the texture of bamboo shoots.

まつたけごはん
Matsutake gohan

栽培できないため高級食材です。香ばしい香りを楽しみます。
Matsutake is a luxury mushroom because it cannot be cultivated. Enjoy its fragrance.

栗ごはん
Kuri gohan

塩で味つけした栗は、海外の方には新しいおいしさです。
Chestnuts seasoned with salt and mixed with rice may be a new taste for many foreign visitors to Japan.

45

赤飯

[*Sekihan* (Rice Cooked with Red Beans)]

もち米と小豆を炊いた、日本のめでたい席の定番ごはんです。

Sekihan cooked with *mochi* rice and red beans is the classic dish for happy occasions in Japan.

小豆から出る汁で赤く色づいたお米の色が、結婚式や誕生日にふさわしい、めでたい色だとされています。通常のごはんのように炊くのではなく、赤飯は蒸し器で蒸して調理します。食べるときには、赤飯の上に黒ゴマ塩を振りかけます。

Rice is cooked with red beans that color the rice red. Red beans are considered appropriate for auspicious occasions such as weddings and birthdays. *Sekihan* is prepared by steaming rice in a steamer unlike regular rice. When eating, why not try sprinkling the dish with salted black sesame seeds.

茶漬け

[*Chazuke*]

ごはんに、あづあづのお茶をかけて食べる軽食です。
A light meal poured hot tea over rice just before eating.

漬物や焼きザケなどをのせて食べます。時間のないときも、手
早くさっと食べることができるので、庶民的な食べ物の代表で
す。今は、タイの刺身やうなぎの佃煮をのせたごはんに、だし
をかけて食べる、贅沢な茶漬けもあります。

Eat *chazuke* with pickles or grilled salmon. It is a traditional,
everyday dish because it can be eaten quickly even when there
is little time for a meal. Nowadays, there is also a luxurious
chazuke that you can eat, where *dashi* broth is poured over
rice topped with sea bream *sashimi* and eel simmered in soy
sauce.

47

雑炊

[*Zosui* (Rice Porridge)]

だしと具で柔らかく炊いたごはんです。
**Rice cooked with *dashi* stock and other ingredients
until it becomes soft.**

だしをたっぷり入れて、野菜や鶏肉などと一緒にやわらかく炊
いたごはんは、やさしい味わいです。消化にもいいので食欲
がないときにも食べられます。鍋料理の最後に残っただしにご
はんを入れ、溶き卵を加えて、雑炊をつくるのも人気があります。
Rice is cooked with plenty of *dashi* stock, vegetables and
chicken until it becomes soft. It has a gentle taste. It is also
suitable for digestive issue, so you can eat it even when you
have no appetite. It is also a popular way to cook porridge by
adding rice in the remaining *dashi* stock of the hot pot with
beaten eggs over the rice.

日本酒

Japanese *Sake*

和食とともに日本酒への関心も高まっています。とくに、飲み心地が軽くフルーティな吟醸酒は西洋の料理にも合うと注目されており、近年、生産量が増えています。日本酒をつくるときは、粒の大きい米が使われます。吟醸酒は、その米を60％以下まで精米し、雑味の元となるたんぱく質を取り除いて作られた特別な日本酒です。日本酒のアルコール度数は15〜16％です。

Interest in *sake* is increasing along with Japanese food. In particular, *ginjo sake*, which is light to drink and fruity, is attracting attention as it goes well with Western cuisine, and its production has been increasing in recent years.

When making *sake*, large grains of rice are used. *Ginjo sake* is a special *sake* made by polishing the rice to 60% or less and removing the protein that causes an odd taste. The alcohol content of *sake* is 15 to 16%.

カレーライス

[Curry and Rice]

とろみのあるカレーをごはんと一緒に食べます。
Try eating thick curry with rice.

日本の子どもが大好きな家庭料理のひとつです。カレーといっても、日本の家庭でつくるカレーは、本場インドのようなたくさんのスパイスを使うスタイルではありません。家庭では市販の「カレールー」を使い、じゃがいも、にんじん、玉ねぎなどの野菜と肉を入れてつくります。シチューのようなとろみがあり、ごはんにかけて食べるのが一般的です。インドでは牛肉を食べないので、ビーフカレーが人気だということに、インドの方はびっくりされます。

Curry and rice is one of the home-cooked dishes that Japanese children love. Curry, which is made at home in Japan, is not like the curry made in India, where a lot of spices are used. In Japan, we buy a ready-made "curry roux" and add meat and vegetables such as potatoes, carrots, and onions at home. Japanese curry is thick like a stew and is usually served on top of rice. Indian people are surprised that beef curry is popular because they don't eat beef in India.

オムライス

[*Omurice*]

チキンライスを薄く焼いた卵でまいた料理です。
A dish of chicken rice covered with a thin omelet.

西洋料理の「オムレツ」と「ライス」を足して、「オムラ
イス」と名づけられた日本で生まれた洋食です。
みじん切りの玉ねぎと小さく切った鶏肉と一緒にごはん
を炒め、トマトケチャップで味つけしたチキンライスを、
薄く焼いた卵で包みます。ラグビーボールのような形をし
ていて、上にケチャップをかけたものが一般的です。

Omurice is a combination of a Western-style dish and
an Eastern-style ingredient that was born in Japan and
named by merging the word "omelet," a Western food,
and the word "rice."

Rice that has been stir-fried with chopped onions
and small pieces of chicken and flavored with tomato
ketchup is wrapped inside a thin omelet. It is shaped
like a rugby ball and usually served with ketchup on
top.

ハヤシライス

[*Hayashi* Rice]

ドミグラスソースで味付けした牛肉を、ごはんと一緒に食べます。

Eat beef seasoned with demiglace sauce with rice.

ハヤシライスのよび名の「ハヤシ」は、英語の「ハッシュ
ドビーフ（牛肉を細切れにするという意味）」が、短くなっ
たものだといわれています。
牛肉の薄切りと玉ねぎを炒めてドミグラスソースで味つけ
し、ごはんにかけて食べます。ハヤシライスは、西洋
料理からヒントを得て、日本独自の進化をとげた料理で
す。

The word "*hayashi*" in the dish called *hayashi* rice
is said to be a shortened version of the English term
"hashed beef" (meaning shredded beef).
Sauté thinly sliced beef and onions, season with
demiglace sauce, and pour over rice. *Hayashi* rice is a
dish inspired by Western cuisine and evolved uniquely
in Japan.

磯部焼き

[*Isobe Yaki*]

焼いたもちにしょうゆにつけ、焼き海苔で巻きます。
Dip grilled *mochi* in soy sauce and wrap it with toasted *nori*.

こんがりと焼いたもちの表面はパリッとし、中はもちもちした食感になります。海外では珍しいので、新しい食感と感じる方も多いかもしれません。焼き海苔の香ばしさがおいしさをひきたてます。軽食としても人気があります。

The surface of the grilled *mochi* is crispy, and the inside has a chewy texture. Since it is rare overseas, many foreigners may find the texture new. The aroma of toasted *nori* is appetizing. It is also popular as a light meal.

きなこもち

[*Kinako Mochi*]

焼いたもちにきなこと砂糖をまぶしたものです。
It is a grilled *mochi* sprinkled with soybean flour and
sugar.

もちは正月に食べることが多いのですが、軽食やおやつにも食
べます。焼いたもちをさっと熱湯にとおし、砂糖ときなこをまぶし
たものです（安倍川もちともよびます）。
Mochi is traditionally eaten during the New Year, and is also
eaten for light meals and snacks. *Kinako mochi* is cooked like
this: First, you grill the *mochi* and then quickly soak it in
hot water. After that, you sprinkle it with sugar and soybean
flour. (Also called *abekawa mochi*.)

もちつきってどうやるの？

How do you do *mochi*-making, *mochi-tsuki*?

もちは普段の食事やおやつとしても食べられていますが、とくに正月などのめでたい行事で用いられてきました。年末には、今でも伝統的な方法でもちつきをする習慣があります。もちになるのは、普通の米より粘り気のあるもち米です。蒸したもち米を臼に入れ、杵でついてもちを作るのです。

Mochi is eaten as a regular meal or snack, but it is eaten especially at New Year and other happy events. At the end of the year, it is still customary to make *mochi* in the traditional way. Glutinous rice, which is stickier than ordinary rice, is used to make *mochi*. *Mochi* is made by putting steamed glutinous rice in a mortar and pounding it with a pestle.

もちつきは二人で行います。一人が杵でつき、もうひとりがついたもちを臼の真ん中に戻す役割をします。掛け声をかけあいながらリズムよく行います。つきたてで熱々のおもちは、やわらかくて格別なおいしさです。

Mochi-tsuki is done by two people, one person pounds with a pestle and the other moves the *mochi* back to the center of the mortar. It has to be done with a good rhythm and shouting to each other. The freshly pounded *mochi* is soft and exceptionally delicious.

Part 3

粉物／麺
Flour-based Foods / Noodles

お好み焼き、たこ焼き、うどんなど、小麦粉でできた食べ物は「粉物」とよびます。

Flour-based foods: *Okonomi-yaki*, *Tako-yaki*, and *Udon* are called "*kona* (flour)-*mono*."

62/

お好み焼き
Okonomi-yaki

64/

広島焼き
Hiroshima-yaki

65/

ねぎ焼き
Negi-yaki

66/

もんじゃ焼き
Monja-yaki

68/

たこ焼き
Tako-yaki

70/

うどん
Udon

72/

そば
Soba

76/

そうめん
Somen

77/

焼きそば
Yakisoba

80/

ラーメン
Ramen

84/

つけ麺
Tsuke-men

85/

冷やし中華
Cold Chinese Noodles

お好み焼き

[*Okonomi-yaki*]

海外の方には 「和風ピザ」 とよばれています。
It is called "Japanese-style pizza" by foreigners.

お好み焼きには大阪スタイルと広島スタイルがあります。
大阪のお好み焼きは、小麦粉、卵、水で作った生地
に刻みキャベツを混ぜます。そこに豚肉の薄切りやエビ
やイカなどの好みの具を入れて鉄板で焼き、熱々のうち
にヘラで切り分けて食べます。ウスターソースにフルーツ
や野菜の甘さと旨みを加えた「お好み焼きソース」を
塗り、好みで青のりやかつお節を振りかけます。

There are two types of *okonomi-yaki*; Osaka-style and
Hiroshima-style. *Okonomi-yaki* in Osaka is made by
mixing dough made from wheat flour, eggs, and water
with chopped cabbage, adding sliced pork, shrimps,
squids and other favorite ingredients, and grilling it
on an iron plate. It is eaten while it is hot by cutting
it with a spatula. Apply "*okonomi-yaki* sauce," which
is a Worcestershire-type sauce, with added sweetness
and *umami* of fruits and vegetables, and sprinkle with
powdered green *nori* and flakes of *katsuo-bushi* (dried
bonito) if wished.

広島焼き

[*Hiroshima-yaki*]

広島スタイルのお好み焼きです。
It is Hiroshima-style *okonomi-yaki*.

広島焼きは、卵の入らない生地を薄く焼き、そこに刻んだキャベツや肉、それに中華麺を入れ、最後に卵を目玉焼きにしてのせるのが特徴です。お好み焼きソースを塗り、青のりやかつお節をかけるのは大阪と同じです。

Hiroshima-yaki is prepared by grilling a thin layer of egg-free dough, adding chopped cabbage, meat, and Chinese noodles, and finally putting a fried egg on the top. Then apply *okonomi-yaki* sauce and sprinkle powdered green *nori* and flakes of *katsuo-bushi* (dried bonito), which is the same as Osaka- style.

ねぎ焼き

[*Negi-yaki*]

青ねぎをたっぷり入れたお好み焼きです。
It is *Okonomi-yaki* with plenty of green onions.

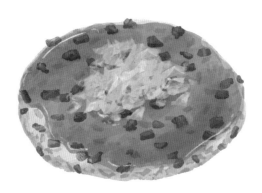

お好み焼きに刻んだ青ねぎを大量に加えたものです。関西地区のねぎ焼きは、牛すじとこんにゃくの煮込みを使い、お好み焼きソースの代わりに、ポン酢（しょうゆに柑橘類の果汁をしぼり、かつお節や昆布の旨みを加えたもの）を使います。

A large amount of chopped green onions are added to this
okonomi-yaki. *Negi-yaki* in the Kansai area contains stewed
beef tendon and *konnyaku*, and instead of *okonomi-yaki* sauce,
ponzu (soy sauce with squeezed citrus juice seasoned with flakes
of *katsuo-bushi* [dried bonito] and kelp) .

もんじゃ焼き

[*Monja-yaki*]

小麦粉を水で溶いて具を入れ、鉄板で焼きながら食べます。

Dissolve the flour in water, add the ingredients, and eat it while grilling on an iron plate.

鉄板で焼き、火が通って固まってきた端の方から「コ
テ」とよばれる小さなヘラで、少しずつすくって食べます。
小麦粉を多めの水で溶いたものに、ソースやしょうゆで
味つけした生地に好みの具を入れて焼きます。
もんじゃ焼きは、昔は駄菓子屋で食べられる手軽な子
どものおやつでしたが、今はイカ、桜エビ、肉、チーズ、
もちなどの具を入れたものが主流です。東京の月島の
名物料理です。

The dough you grill is made by adding a large amount
of water to the flour and seasoning with sauce or soy
sauce, then mixing in your favorite ingredients. Grill
this snack on an iron plate and eat by scooping it up
little by little with a small spatula called a "*kote*" from
the edge that has been cooked by the heat.
Monja-yaki used to be made with simple ingredients,
a casual snack for children to eat at a candy store.
Nowadays, the *monja-yaki* that is prepared with
ingredients such as squids, *sakura* shrimps, meat, cheese,
and *mochi* has become a specialty dish of Tsukishima in
Tokyo.

たこ焼き

[*Tako-yaki*]

溶いた小麦粉に卵を混ぜ、タコを入れて丸く焼きます。
Make the dough by adding an egg to the mixture of water and flour, put the octopus in the dough and bake it in a cooker with round-shaped molds.

たこ焼き器（一口サイズの球型の穴がたくさんある鉄製
の型）に生地を流し込み、タコの切り身を入れて焼き
あげます。あつあつのうちに、ソース、マヨネーズ、青のり、
かつお節をかけて食べるのが一般的です。縁日の屋台
やたこ焼き屋で買うことができます。
大阪名物としてよく知られており、大阪のソウルフードと
いわれます。大阪の人は、ほとんどの人が自宅にたこ焼
き器を持っているといわれています。

Pour the dough into a *tako-yaki* cooker (an iron mold
with many bite-sized spheres), add the chopped octopus
and bake. It is common to eat *tako-yaki* with sauce,
mayonnaise, green *nori*, and flakes of *katsuo-bushi* (dried
bonito) while they are hot.

You can buy them at fair stalls and *tako-yaki* shops. It
is well known as an Osaka specialty and is called Osaka'
s soul food. It is said that most people in Osaka have a
tako-yaki cooker at home.

うどん

[*Udon*]

小麦粉を塩水でこねて薄くのばし、細く切った麺です。
Noodles made by kneading wheat flour with salt water,
spreading it thinly, and cutting into thin noodles.

かつお節や昆布のだしに、みりんとしょうゆで味つけした
つゆに、ゆでたてのうどんを入れた温かいうどんと、冷
やしてつゆにつける冷やしうどんがあります。もちもちした
食感としっかりした弾力性は「こし」とよばれ、うどんの
特徴のひとつです。

うどんが有名な地域はいくつかありますが、香川県は「う
どん県」というニックネームがあるほど有名です。作り方
を学べる教室も開かれています。

There are two types of *udon* noodles: hot *udon* noodles
are served freshly boiled in a hot broth made from
katsuo-bushi (dried bonito) and kelp seasoned with
mirin and soy sauce, and cold *udon* noodles are served
with a cold dipping sauce. The chewy texture and
firm elasticity is known as "*koshi*," and is one of the
characteristics of *udon* noodles.

There are several areas where *udon* is famous, and
among them is Kagawa prefecture which is known by its
nickname, "*udon* prefecture." They even have cooking
classes where you can learn how to make them.

そば

[*Soba*]

そば粉に小麦粉などを足し、水でこねて細く切った麺です。
Noodles made by adding wheat flour to buckwheat
flour, kneading with water and cutting.

温かいそばも冷やしたそばも、どちらも人気があります。
冷やしてざるにのせ、刻み海苔をかけたそばは「ざるそ
ば」とよばれ、冷たいつゆに、少しずつ入れて食べます。
そば粉には、健康によい栄養素がたくさん含まれている
ことが知られています。小麦粉や卵やナガイモを加えて
こねるのは、デンプンが少なく、つなぎが必要だからで
す。小麦粉を使わずにそば粉だけでつくったものを「十
割そば」とよびます。

Both hot and cold *soba* are popular. *Soba* that has been
chilled and sprinkled with thinly cut *nori* is called "*zaru
soba*" and is eaten by dipping it into cold broth little by
little.

Buckwheat flour is known to be rich in healthy
nutrients. Flour, eggs and yam are added to buckwheat
flour and kneaded because buckwheat flour is low in
starch and needs a binder. The noodles that are made
with only buckwheat flour without using wheat flour are
called "100% buckwheat *soba*."

うどんとそばの種類いろいろ

[Types of *Udon* and *Soba*]

月見うどん・そば
Tsukimi udon / soba

生卵を入れたもの。黄身が満月に見えるので「月見」とよびます。

Udon or *soba* with a raw egg as the topping are called "*Tsukimi*," meaning moon-viewing. The reason for the name "*Tukimi udon / soba*" is that the yolk looks like a full moon.

きつねうどん・そば
Kitsune udon / soba

甘辛く煮た油揚げをのせたもの。昔は、油揚げはきつねの好物と考えられていました。

Topped with sweet soy-flavored fried *tofu*. The name originated from fried *tofu*, which was considered a favorite food of foxes in the olden days.

たぬきうどん・そば
Tanuki udon / soba

天かすをのせたもの。きつねに対し、たぬきとよばれます。

These noodles have *tenkasu* (*tempura* scraps) on top. The reason for the name "*tanuki*" (racoon) is to show the difference from *kitsune* (fox) noodles.

カレーうどん・そば
Curry *udon* / *soba*

だしで割ったカレーをかけて食べます。
Eat with curry-flavored *dashi* broth.

天ぷらうどん・そば
Tempura udon* / *soba

エビやかき揚げなどの天ぷらを
のせて食べます。
Eat with *tempura* such as
shrimp *tempura* or with
kakiage on top of the noodles.

「きつね」「たぬき」のネーミング
Naming of "*Kitsune* (fox)" and "*Tanuki* (raccoon)"

関東エリアと関西エリア
で指すものが逆になりま
す。「きつね」は関東で
は油揚げをのせたもの、
関西では天かすのことで
す。「たぬき」は関東で
は天かすをのせたもの、
関西では油揚げのことで
す。

The names indicate the opposite
toppings for *udon* in the Kanto area
and the Kansai area. The "*kitsune*"
toppings in the Kanto region are fried
tofu, whereas they are *tenkasu* (*tempura
scraps*) in the Kansai region. The
"*tanuki*" toppings in the Kanto region
are *tenkasu*, but they are fried *tofu* in
the Kansai region.

そうめん

[*Somen*]

1.3㎜以下の太さに切って乾燥させた細い麺です。

Thin noodles cut to a thickness of 1.3 mm or less and dried.

夏の暑い日に食べるのに適しています。ゆでたらすぐに冷やして、冷たいつゆにつけて食べます。観光地では、「流しそうめん」が楽しめるところもあります。竹筒をつなぎ、水とともにそうめんを流し、箸でとって、つゆにつけて食べます。

Suitable for eating on hot summer days. Immediately after boiling, cool and dip them in cold soup to eat. In some tourist spots, you can enjoy "*Nagashi Somen*." At the spots, local people connect bamboo tubes, let the *somen* flow down with the water, and you can pick them up with chopsticks, and dip them in soup to eat.

焼きそば

[*Yakisoba*]

中華麺をソースや塩などで味つけして炒めた料理です。
Fried Chinese noodles seasoned with sauce or salt.

中華麺をキャベツや玉ねぎなどの野菜や肉と一緒に炒めて、焼きそばソースや塩などで味つけをします。鉄板の上で調理できるため、縁日の屋台の定番になっています。家庭料理としても人気があります。

Fried Chinese noodles with vegetables such as cabbage and onions, and meat, seasoned with *yakisoba* sauce or salt. Since this dish can be cooked on an iron plate, it has become a popular menu item of fair stalls. It is popular for home cooking too.

日本のスパイス

Japanese spices

わさび
Wasabi

鼻にぬける辛味があります。日本特産の
もので自生していますが、市場では栽培
したものが売られています。チューブのわさびは加工品です。

Wasabi has a pungent taste that goes through your nose. It
is a Japanese specialty and grows naturally, but cultivated
ones are sold in the market. The *wasabi* you get in a tube is
a processed product.

山椒
Sansho / Japanese pepper

日本の山に自生する山椒の木の実を乾燥させて粉にし、独
特の香りと辛味があります。山椒の新芽（木の芽）も彩りと
して添えられます。

Sansho is a kind of Japanese pepper that
grows naturally in the mountains of
Japan. Its fruits are used as spice when
they are dried and powdered. They
have a unique aroma and spiciness.
Sprouts of *sansho* are used as garnish.

七味唐辛子
Shichimi-togarashi

唐辛子をメインに、山椒、麻の実、
黒胡麻、陳皮、菜辛、生姜など、
七つのスパイスをまぜたもの。地方
や店によって調合が変わります。

A spice mainly of red chili pepper, mixed with seven
spices: *sansho*, hemp seeds, black sesame, dried citrus peel,
rapeseeds, and ginger. The formulation varies depending on
the region and store.

柚子胡椒
Yuzu pepper

柚子の産地で生まれました。刻んだ青柚子の皮、青唐辛子
に塩を加えてすりつぶします。さわやかな香りと辛味が特徴
です。

Originally, it was made in the
yuzu production area. Add salt to
chopped green *yuzu* peel and green
pepper and grind. It features a
refreshing aroma and spiciness.

ラーメン

[*Ramen*]

中国発祥の麺が、日本でさまざまな進化をとげました。
Noodles originating in China have undergone various
evolutions in Japan.

ラーメンには、いろいろな味があり、定番のしょうゆ味は、鶏ガラをベースに、かつお節や煮干しで風味をつけ、しょうゆで味をつけます。

海外の方に人気が高いのは、「豚骨ラーメン」です。豚骨だしをベースにしたスープが特徴で、麺のゆで加減で固さを選べたり、麺だけ追加する「替え玉」ができたりする店もあります。豚骨ラーメンは博多名物で知られていますが、日本各地に「ご当地ラーメン」があるので、食べ比べを楽しむのもおすすめです。

There are various *ramen* flavors, but the standard soy sauce *ramen* mainly uses chicken broth and a broth of dried sardines and flakes of *katsuo-buahi* (dried bonito), and is seasoned with soy sauce.

"*Tonkotsu ramen*" is very popular with foreigners. It features pork bone broth, and you can choose the firmness of the noodles which is adjusted by the boiling time, or after eating the noodles, you can add "*kaedama*" or a refill of noodles. Pork bone *ramen* is known as a Hakata specialty, but there are "local *ramens*" all over Japan, so it is recommended to try and compare them.

ラーメンの種類いろいろ

[Types of *Ramen*]

しょうゆラーメン
Shoyu ramen

元祖といわれる定番の味です。
「中華そば」ともよばれます。
A classic taste that is said to be
the origin of *ramen*. It is also
called "*chuka-soba*."

みそラーメン
Miso ramen

野菜と肉をみそで炒めてのせ
ます。札幌の名物です。
Add vegetables and meat
stir-fried with *miso* on top
the of *ramen*. This dish is a
specialty of Sapporo.

塩ラーメン
Shio ramen

塩だれで味付けした、さっぱりと
した味わいです。

Ramen with a refreshing taste,
seasoned with salt.

ご当地ラーメン
Local specialty *ramens*

日本の各地に、特徴のある
ご当地ラーメンがあります。
上で紹介した以外に、しょ
うゆ魚介系の濃厚なスープ
の喜多方ラーメンや、しょ
うゆ味極細縮れ麺の高山
ラーメンも有名です。

There are unique "local *ramens*"
all over Japan. Kitakata *ramen*
with a rich soup using soy sauce
and seafood broth, and Takayama
ramen using soy sauce flavor soup
with ultra-thin curly noodle are
also famous other than above.

つけ麺

[*Tsuke-men*]

冷やした中華麺を、熱いつゆにつけて食べます。
Eat chilled Chinese noodles by dipping them in hot
soup.

ゆでた後、冷水でしめた麺を、濃いめに味つけされた熱いつ
ゆにつけて食べます。麺そのものの食感やコシを楽しむことがで
きます。麺を食べ終わってから、魚介や鶏の熱いスープを頼
めば、スープのおいしさも味わえます。
After boiling the noodles, chill them in cold water. Then eat by
dipping in a thick hot soup.
First, you can enjoy the texture and elasticity of the noodles
themselves. Then, after eating the noodles, if you have ordered
hot soup flavored with seafood or chicken, you can then enjoy
the soup's deliciousness.

冷やし中華

[Cold Chinese Noodles]

冷やした中華麺に具をのせて、甘酸っぱいタレをかけます。
Put the ingredients on the chilled Chinese noodles and
pour sweet and sour sauce.

夏にぴったりのさわやかな味の麺料理です。 ゆでた中華麺を
冷水で冷やして皿に盛り、その上に卵焼き、キュウリ、蒸し鶏、
紅しょうがの細切りなどの具をのせ、甘酢ダレ（または、ごまダ
レ）をかけて食べます。

A refreshing noodle dish perfect for summer. Boil the Chinese
noodles, chill them in cold water, and serve on a plate, topped
with ingredients such as omelet, cucumber, steamed chicken
and shredded pickled ginger, and then eat with sweet and sour
sauce (or sesame sauce).

日本の調理器具

Japanese cooking utensils

和包丁
Japanese knife

和包丁が洋包丁と大きく違うのは、洋包丁が刃の表と裏に刃がある両刃であり、ほとんどの和包丁は片側のみに刃がついている片刃である点です。和包丁は、手前に引いて使い、刺身などの切り口が滑らかになることが特徴です。おみやげとして和包丁を買う海外の方も増えています。日本人シェフの見事な包丁さばきを見たり、日本の侍の刀のイメージが影響したりしているようです。

The big differences between Japanese knives and Western ones are that most Japanese knives are single-edged while Western ones are double-edged and Japanese knives are used by pulling them toward you to cut things. By using the single-edged blade, the cut end of *sashimi* becomes smooth. An increasing number of overseas visitors are buying Japanese knives as souvenirs. It seems that this is influenced by the Japanese chef's excellent kitchen knife handling and the image of the Japanese *samurai* sword.

かつお節削り器
Katsuobushi shaver

かつお節を削る体験も海外の方に人気があります。日本ならではの道具として、削り器をおみやげに選ばれる方もいます。

The experience of shaving bonito flakes is also popular for overseas visitors. Some people choose the shaver, a unique tool of Japan, as a souvenir.

サメ皮のおろし金
Shark skin grater

めずらしいと注目されます。サメ皮は目が非常に細かいため、わさびをおろすと空気をふくみ、辛さだけでなく微かな甘味が感じられます。

People find this grater a unique tool. *Wasabi* grated with it has not only spiciness, but also slight sweetness because some air is kept within it.

Part 4

煮物／蒸し物
Boiled / Steamed Food

鍋物はいろいろな種類があります。鍋料理のスタイルは
世界では珍しいです。
Various types of meals are cooked in a pot at the table.
This is a unique style of cooking in the world.

90 /

すき焼き
Suki-yaki

92 /

しゃぶしゃぶ
Shabu-shabu

94 /

寄せ鍋
Yose-nabe

95 /

鶏の水炊き
Tori no Mizutaki
(*Mizutaki* Chicken)

98 /

湯豆腐
Yudofu
(Boiled *Tofu*)

100 /

おでん
Oden

102 /

肉じゃが
Nikujaga
(Meat and Potatoes)

103 /

サバの味噌煮
Saba no Misoni
(Simmered Mackerel in *Miso*)

104 /

茶碗蒸し
Chawan-mushi
(Savory Cup Custard)

すき焼き

[*Suki-yaki*]

薄切り牛肉、野菜、焼き豆腐を甘辛く煮て溶き卵につけます。
Cook thinly sliced beef, vegetables, and *yaki-dofu* with sweetened soy sauce and dip them in beaten raw egg.

西洋文化の影響を強く受けた明治時代（1868 〜
1912 年）に、日本でも牛肉を食べるようになりました。
その頃にうまれた料理で、海外で人気になった和食の
第一号であるともいえます。

調理法は地域で異なります。関東は鍋で温めた「割り
下」という調味料に具を入れて煮ます。関西は先に牛
肉を焼いて食べ、そのあとに野菜などを入れます。生卵
が苦手という海外の方には、生卵を溶いたソースに熱
い肉を入れてからめ、半熟卵にするのがおすすめです。

During the Meiji era (1868-1912), which was strongly
influenced by Western culture, beef began to be eaten
in Japan. *Sukiyaki* is a dish born around that time and
can be said to be the first Japanese dish that became
popular overseas.

Cooking methods vary from region to region. In the
Kanto area, ingredients are simmered in a sauce called
"*warishita*" that has been warmed in a pot. In the
Kansai area, beef is grilled and eaten first, and then
vegetables are added. For foreigners who are not used
to eating raw eggs, you may recommend that they put
the hot meat in the beaten raw egg so that the egg will
become like a soft-boiled egg.

しゃぶしゃぶ

[*Shabu-shabu*]

海外の方に、「和風フォンデュ」とよばれて親しまれています。
**Popular with foreigners and known as "Japanese
fondue."**

昆布だしをとった湯の中に、薄切りの牛肉（または豚肉）を入れて火を通し、タレをつけて食べます。「しゃぶしゃぶ」という不思議な響きの名前は、お湯の中に肉を入れるときの擬音からきています。肉だけではなく野菜や豆腐などの具も加えます。タレには、ごまダレやポン酢ダレがあり、赤唐辛子と大根を一緒におろした「紅葉おろし」や刻みねぎを加えます。海外の方には、和風フォンデュは、チーズやオイルを使わないのでヘルシーだと喜ばれます。

Put thinly sliced beef (or pork) in hot water flavored with kelp, cook it, and eat it by dipping in a sauce. The name "*shabu-shabu*" strangely sounds like the onomatopoeia of the sound of dipping meat in hot water. Add not only meat but also vegetables and *tofu*. For dipping, there are sesame sauce and *ponzu* sauce, and you can also add "*momiji-oroshi*" (grated *daikon* and red pepper) and chopped green onions. Foreigners will appreciate that Japanese-style fondue is healthy because it does not use cheese or oil.

寄せ鍋

[*Yose-nabe*]

さまざまな具材を入れたカジュアルな鍋料理です。
A casual hot pot dish with various ingredients.

大きな鍋に肉や海産物、たっぷりの野菜やきのこ、豆腐など
を入れて、味のついただしで煮ます。大勢の人で鍋を囲んで、
おたまで取り分け、にぎやかに食べます。地方によって好みの
具材があり、関東では海鮮類、九州では鶏肉、四国では豚
肉が好まれています。

Put meat, seafood, plenty of vegetables, mushrooms, *tofu*, etc.
in a large pot and simmer with flavored broth. A large number
of people surround the pot, sharing the food using a ladle and
enjoy eating together. There are favorite ingredients in each
region: seafood in Kanto, chicken in Kyushu, and pork in
Shikoku.

鶏の水炊き

[*Tori no Mizutaki* (*Mizutaki* Chicken)]

鶏肉、野菜、きのこ、豆腐を煮て、ポン酢をつけて食べます。
Simmer chicken, vegetables, mushrooms and *tofu*, and
eat by dipping in *ponzu* sauce.

鶏肉のだしがきいた鍋です。鍋には調味料を入れず、昆布を
入れた水で具材を煮込むので「水炊き」とよばれています。
煮たあとに、タレをつけて食べます。ポン酢に、大根と唐辛子
をすりおろした「紅葉おろし」という薬味を加えるのが定番です。
Mizutaki is a hot pot made with chicken stock. It is called
"*mizutaki*" because the ingredients are simmered in water
containing kelp without adding seasonings to the pot. When
the ingredients are cooked, eat them by dipping in a *ponzu*
sauce. Usually a condiment called "*momiji-oroshi*," (grated
daikon and pepper), is added to the sauce.

スモーフードと親しまれる「ちゃんこ鍋」

"Chanko nabe," known as *"Sumo* food"

相撲部屋では、稽古の前には食事をしないほうがいい
ので、朝ごはんは食べません。朝稽古をした後に、力
士たちがみんなで一緒に「ちゃんこ鍋」を食べる習慣
があります。ちゃんこ鍋は具がたっぷりと入っています。
激しい運動をした後に栄養価の高い食事をすると、体
重が増えやすく、力士としての体づくりに効果的なのだ
そうです。

In the *sumo* stable, wrestlers don't eat breakfast because
they think that they should not eat before training.
After practicing in the morning, it is customary for
them to eat *"chanko nabe"* together. *Chanko nabe*
contains plenty of ingredients. Eating a nutritious diet
after strenuous exercise makes it easier for them to gain
weight and is effective in building a body suitable for a
sumo wrestler.

たっぷりの出汁に、野菜と豆腐、肉や魚を入れて、味噌や醤油で味付けをするちゃんこ鍋は、一般の人にも人気の高い鍋のひとつです。相撲の試合が行われる両国国技館のまわりには、おいしいちゃんこ鍋の専門店がたくさん並んでいます。

Chanko nabe, which is made by adding vegetables, *tofu*, meat and fish to a generous amount of *dashi* stock and seasoning with *miso* or soy sauce, is also popular among the general public. Around the Ryogoku Kokugikan where *sumo* tournaments are held, there are many *chanko nabe* specialty restaurants.

湯豆腐

[*Yudofu* (Boiled *Tofu*)]

豆腐そのもののおいしさが味わえます。

You can enjoy the deliciousness of the *tofu* itself.

昆布を入れた湯で、豆腐を煮るシンプルな料理です。
煮たあとに、しょうゆ、酒、みりん、だしなどを合わせた
タレ（または、ポン酢）につけて食べます。
近年、豆腐は海外でもヘルシーなたんぱく質源として
注目されていますが、味つけをしてソテーで食べる方が
多いようです。淡白すぎて味がないと感じる海外の方も
いますが、湯豆腐は、豆腐そのものの、ほのかな大豆
の香りと風味のおいしさを味わえる料理です。

Yudofu is a simple dish made by boiling *tofu* in hot
water with kelp. After cooking, scoop it out and dip it
in a sauce consisting of soy sauce, *sake*, *mirin*, and *dashi*
stock (or *ponzu* sause).

Tofu has been attracting attention as a healthy source
of protein overseas in recent years, but it seems that
many people outside of Japan eat it by sautéing it with
some seasoning. Some foreigners feel that *tofu* is too
plain and tasteless, but with *yudofu* you can enjoy the
delicate aroma of soybeans and the flavor of *tofu* itself.

おでん

[Oden]

しょうゆなどで味つけしただしで、具を煮込む料理です。
**Various ingredients are stewed in a broth seasoned with
soy sauce.**

しょうゆ、みりん、塩で味つけした、たっぷりのだしで、厚めに切った大根、こんにゃく、がんもどき、練り物などを煮込んだ料理です。「がんもどき」は、くずした豆腐に刻んだ野菜を加えて、丸めて揚げたものです。「練り物」は魚のすり身を使った製品で、ちくわやはんぺんなど、いろいろな種類があります。

あつあつのおでんは、寒い冬の日に食べることが多い家庭料理のひとつですが、居酒屋や屋台でも人気のあるメニューです。

Ingredients such as thickly sliced *daikon*, *konnyaku*, *ganmodoki*, and fish cakes are stewed in a generous amount of *dashi* stock seasoned with soy sauce, *mirin*, and salt. "*Ganmodoki*" is made by adding chopped vegetables to squashed *tofu*, and then fried. "*Nerimono*" is made using minced fish meat, and there are various kinds of *nerimono* such as *chikuwa* and *hanpen* as well. Hot *oden* is one of those home-cooked dishes that are often eaten on cold winter days, but it is also a popular menu item at *izakayas* and food stalls.

肉じゃが

[*Nikujaga* (Meat and Potatoes)]

薄切りの牛肉と野菜を煮た、手軽でおいしい家庭料理です。

A simple and delicious home-cooked dish made by simmering sliced beef and vegetables.

薄切りの牛肉（または豚肉）とじゃがいも、人参、玉ねぎを炒めてから、だし（または水）を入れ、しょうゆ、砂糖、酒を加えて、一緒に煮込むだけでできあがります。古くから人気の家庭料理のひとつで、代表的な「おふくろの味」です。

Fry sliced beef (or pork) and potatoes with carrots and onions, add *dashi* stock (or water), soy sauce, sugar, and *sake*, and simmer together. *Nikujaga* is one of the all-time favorite home-cooked dishes, and it is a typical of "Mom's home cooking."

サバの味噌煮

[*Saba no Misoni* (Simmered Mackerel in *Miso*)]

サバの切り身を甘めの味噌で煮た、定番の煮魚料理です。

A classic fish dish made by simmering mackerel fillets in sweet *miso*.

味噌、しょうゆ、みりん、酒などで味つけし、ショウガの薄切りを加えて煮ます。ショウガと一緒に煮ることでサバの臭みをおさえます。ねぎの白い部分をせん切りにした「白髪ねぎ」をかざることもあります。

Season with *miso*, soy sauce, *mirin*, *sake*, etc., add thin slices of ginger and simmer. The addition of ginger suppresses the smell of mackerel. In some cases, "*shiraga-negi*," the thinly sliced white part of the green onion, is placed on the fish.

茶碗蒸し

[*Chawan-mushi* (Savory Cup Custard)]

カスタードプリンに似ていますが、蒸した卵の料理です。
A dish of steamed eggs similar to custard pudding.

具を入れた器に、溶いた卵と、しょうゆ、みりん、塩で
味つけしただし（卵の3倍の量）を混ぜたものを入れて、
蒸したものです。だしを混ぜた卵は、ザルで濾すので、
食べたときの口当たりがなめらかです。具は、鶏肉、
海老、銀杏などが一般的です。色どりがきれいな三つ
葉を上にのせてかざることもあります。海外の方には、「甘
くないプリン」だといわれることもありますが、スイーツよ
りも、蒸した卵のスープと表現するほうが、イメージに
近いかもしれません。

Beaten eggs mixed with *dashi* stock seasoned with soy
sauce, *mirin*, and salt (three times the amount of eggs)
is poured into a cup together with ingredients.
Eggs mixed with *dashi* stock are strained with a
colander, so it is smooth to taste. The common
ingredients are chicken, shrimps, and ginkgo nuts.
For decoration, trefoil is often placed on top. Some
foreigners call it "unsweetened pudding," but it may be
more accurate to describe it as a steamed egg soup than
a sweet dessent dish.

箸の正しい使い方

How to use chopsticks

1. 上の箸を、鉛筆を持つように指で持ちます。
1. Hold the top chopstick just like holding a pencil.

↓

2. もう一本の箸を薬指の先と親指の付け根で固定します。
2. The other stick is fixed with the tip of the ring finger and the base of the thumb.

↓

3. 動かすのは上の箸だけです。
3. Make sure that you move only the chopstick on the top.

箸の間違った持ち方

Wrong way of holding chopsticks

下記のイラストのように、2本の箸をいっしょに握るような
持ち方は間違いです。正しい持ち方で箸を使うと、動
かしやすくなります。

As shown in the illustration below, it is not right to
hold the two chopsticks together. Knowing the correct
way to hold them will make it easier to use them.

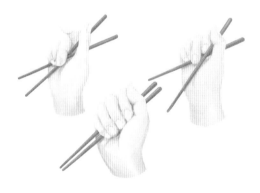

Part 5

揚げ物／焼き物
Deep-fried / Grilled Food

揚げ物と焼き物は、和食のメインディッシュといえます。
Deep-fried dishes and grilled dishes are the main
course of Japanese cuisine.

110/

天ぷら
Tempura

114/

とんかつ
Ton-katsu (Pork Cutlet)

116/

メンチかつ
Menchi-katsu
(Ground-meat Cutlet)

118/

鶏のからあげ
Tori no Karaage (Deep-fried Marinated Chicken)

120/

コロッケ
Korokke (Potato Croquette)

124/

だし巻き卵
Dashimaki Tamago

126/

照り焼きチキン
Teriyaki Chicken

128/

豚肉のしょうが焼き
Butaniku no Shogayaki
(Grilled Pork in Ginger)

130/

和風ハンバーグ
Japanese-style
Hamburger Steak

134/

焼き鳥
Yakitori

136/

鉄板焼き
Teppan-yaki

138/

炉ばた焼き
Robata-yaki

天ぷら

[*Tempura*]

魚介や肉、野菜などに衣をつけて揚げた料理です。
Deep-fried seafood, meat, vegetables.

天ぷらは揚げ方が難しく、衣のサクサクとしたおいしい
食感をつくるにはコツが必要です。食材はさまざまで、
お店では「盛り合わせ」を注文すると、ひとつのお皿（ま
たはかご）に、さまざまな種類が盛られて出されます。
天ぷら専門店では、好きな食材を選んで注文することも
できます。とくに人気があるのは、エビの天ぷらです。
16 世紀にスペイン、ポルトガルの宣教師が日本に伝え
たのが、天ぷらのはじまりだといわれていますが、今で
は代表的な和食のひとつです。

Tempura is difficult to fry, and you need to know
how to make the batter crispy and delicious. There
are various ingredients, and if you order "*moriawase*
(assorted *tempura*)" at a restaurant, you can have a
variety of *tempura* on one plate (or in a basket). At
a specialty *tempura* restaurant, you can also order
à la carte and choose your favorite ingredients. An
especially popular choice is shrimp *tempura*. It is
said that *tempura* was first introduced to Japan by
missionaries from Spain and Portugal in the 16th
century. However, it is now one of the typical Japanese
cuisines.

天ぷらの具材いろいろ

[Types of *Tempura*]

魚介類
Fish and seafood

エビのほかにも、イカや白身魚
などが人気です。
Besides shrimps, squids and
white fish are also popular.

野菜
Vegetables

ナス、マイタケ、サツマイモ、カ
ボチャなどがあります。
Eggplants, *maitake*
mushrooms, sweet potatoes,
pumpkins, etc.

肉
Meat

鶏肉が人気です。「とり天（ま
たは、かしわ天）」とよばれます。
Chicken *tempura* is popular. It
is called "*tori-ten*" or "*kashiwa-
ten.*"

かき揚げ
Kakiage

魚介類や、野菜などを細かく切ったものを、小麦粉を水でといた衣
でつなぎ、ひとつにまとめたものを油で揚げます。小エビ、貝柱、玉
ねぎ、三つ葉などが人気の具材です。かき揚げをごはんにのせ、つ
ゆをかけた「かき揚げ丼」も人気の高い料理です。

Finely chopped seafood and
vegetables are mixed with batter
made of flour and water and
deep-fried in one cluster.Shrimps,
bivalve mollusks, onions, and
trefoil are popular ingredients.
"*Kakiage-don*," which is made
by putting *kakiage* on rice and
pouring sweet soy sauce over it, is
also a popular dish.

とんかつ

[*Ton-katsu* (Pork Cutlet)]

豚肉に小麦粉、溶き卵、パン粉をつけて揚げたもの。
Pork coated in flour, beaten egg and bread crumbs and
deep-fried.

厚切りの豚肉（ロース肉、またはヒレ肉）に、衣をつ
けて油で揚げます。外の衣はサクッとした食感、中の肉
はジューシーになるのが、人気の理由のひとつです。
あつあつのとんかつに、「とんかつソース」とよばれると
ろみのあるソースをかけ、からしを好みで加えて食べる
のが一般的です。大根おろしをのせ、ポン酢をつけて
食べることもあります。付け合わせには、千切りキャベツ
をたっぷりと添えるのが定番です。西洋料理のカツレツ
に、ヒントを得てつくられた和食です。

Batter thick slices of pork (loin or fillet) and deep-fry.
One of the reasons for its popularity is that the outside
coating is crispy and the meat inside is juicy.

It is common to eat the hot *tonkatsu* with a thick sauce
called "*tonkatsu* sauce" and add mustard as well if
desired. You may also like to eat it with grated *daikon*
and *ponzu* sauce. It is standard to garnish with plenty
of shredded cabbage. It is a Japanese cuisine inspired
by Western-style cutlets.

メンチかつ

[*Menchi-katsu* (Ground-meat Cutlet)]

合いびき肉と玉ねぎを混ぜ、衣をつけて揚げたもの。
A mixture of ground meat and onions, battered and fried.

牛肉と豚肉の合いびき肉に、玉ねぎのみじん切りを混
ぜ合わせ、丸めて平たい形にし、小麦粉、溶き卵、
パン粉の順にまぶして、揚げたものです。観光地では、
食べ歩きのできる気軽なスナックとしても人気を集めてい
ます。

日本のパン粉は、大きめで粒のサイズがそろっているた
め、西洋のパン粉より、揚げ物がサクっと揚がると海外
シェフの間で評判になりました。海外でも PANKO とよ
ばれて普及しています。

Menchi-katsu is made by mixing chopped onion with
ground beef and pork, rolling the mixture into a flat
round shape, coating it with flour, beaten egg, and
bread crumbs in that order, and then frying. It is
gaining popularity in tourist areas as a casual snack
that you can eat while walking.

Japanese bread crumbs are large and have the same
grain size, so when they are cooked they are crispier
than Western bread crumbs. This is why Japanese
bread crumbs have become popular among overseas
chefs. They are called "*panko*" and are now widely
used overseas.

鶏のからあげ

[*Tori no Karaage* (Deep-fried Marinated Chicken)]

しょうゆで味つけした鶏肉に粉をまぶして揚げます。
Sprinkle flour on chicken marinated with soy sauce and
deep-fry.

大人も子どもも大好きな定番の家庭料理であり、定食屋や居酒屋でも人気の高い料理です。

一口サイズに切った鶏肉（もも肉、または胸肉）を、酒、しょうが汁、しょうゆに 30 分ほど漬けこみ、はじめに下味をつけておくのが、日本スタイルのフライドチキンです。

好みに合わせ、レモンをしぼったり、マヨネーズをつけて食べることもあります。

A classic home-cooked dish that both adults and children love, *tori no karaage* is also a popular dish at diners and *izakayas*.

This Japanese-style fried chicken is prepared by marinating bite-sized chicken (thigh or breast meat) pieces in *sake*, ginger juice, and soy sauce for about 30 minutes.

You may also wish to add squeezed lemon juice or mayonnaise to it to your liking.

コロッケ

[*Korokke* (Potato Croquette)]

ゆでてつぶしたジャガイモをまるめ、衣をつけて揚げたもの
です。
Boiled and mashed potatoes are shaped into rolls then
battered and fried.

おやつとしても、おかずとしても人気の高い料理です。
西洋料理のクロケットを日本風にアレンジしたものが定
着し、日本料理として知られるようになりました。
ゆでてつぶしたジャガイモに、みじん切りにした玉ねぎと
ひき肉を炒めたものを混ぜてまるめ、小麦粉、溶き卵、
パン粉の順で衣をつけて揚げます。外の衣はサクッと、
中のジャガイモはホクホクとした食感です。

Popular as a snack and a main dish, this Japanese-style
version of Western croquettes has become common
and is known as a Japanese food.
To make *korokke*, first, you boil and mash potatoes,
mix them with chopped onions and stir-fried minced
meat. Next, you make the mixture into rolls and dip in
flour, then beaten eggs and finally bread crumbs, and
then deep-fry. The outside coating is crispy, and the
potato inside is hot and flaky.

日本の弁当

Japanese *bento* (box lunches)

弁当箱の半分にごはん、もう半分におかずを入れるスタイルが一般的です。卵焼きや、から揚げは人気のおかずです。レタスやミニトマトを入れて色どりをよくします。今では、コンビニなどで手軽に弁当を買うこともできますが、栄養バランスの良い手製の弁当を、通学や通勤に持っていく人も増えています。

It is common to put rice in half of the *bento* box and side dishes in the other half. Omelet and fried chicken are popular side dishes. Add lettuce and cherry tomatoes to make it colorful. Nowadays, you can easily buy *bento* at convenience stores, but more and more people take homemade *bento* with a good nutritional balance to schools and offices.

弁当いろいろ

Types of *bento*

キャラ弁
Chara-ben

アニメの人気キャラクターなどを食べ物で形づくった弁当のことです。ブログや YouTube などを通じて、海外の方の認知度が上がりました。

Chara-ben is *bento* decorated with the designs of popular animation characters using food. *Chara-ben* has become more widely known overseas through blogs and YouTube.

駅弁
Eki-ben

駅で売られる弁当は、電車の旅の楽しみのひとつです。デパートなどで全国有名駅弁販売の企画をしていることもあります。

Bento sold at stations are one of the pleasures of traveling by train. There are also events to sell famous *eki-ben* nationwide at places like department stores.

だし巻き卵

[*Dashimaki Tamago*]

溶き卵にだしを加え、薄く焼きながら巻きます。
Rolled thin omelet made of beaten egg mixed with
dashi **stock.**

西洋料理のオムレツとの大きな違いは、溶き卵にだし（卵の約3割の量）を加えていることです。しょうゆ、みりんで味をつけた卵液をつくり、長方形の卵焼き専用のフライパンで焼きます。
あたためたフライパンに、卵液を少しずつ入れ、焼き上がった部分を箸で引き寄せ、奥から手前に向かって巻きます。再度、卵液を加え、焼いては巻くという工程を繰り返します。だし巻き卵の作り方を学べる和食の料理教室は、海外の方にとても人気があります。

The big difference from the Western omelet is that the *dashi* stock (the amount is about 30% of the egg) is added to the beaten egg. The egg mixture seasoned with soy sauce and *mirin* is cooked in a rectangular frying pan, specially designed for this dish.

Pour the egg mixture little by little into the heated frying pan, roll up the cooked part with chopsticks and move it toward you. Repeat the process of adding egg mixture, cooking and rolling. Japanese cooking classes that teach how to make *dashimaki tamago* are extremely popular with foreigners.

照り焼きチキン

[*Teriyaki* Chicken]

しょうゆやみりんを混ぜたタレをからめて焼いた鶏肉です。
Grilled chicken cooked with sauce mixed with soy sauce and *mirin*.

「照り焼き」は、甘辛いタレをからめて、照り（ツヤ）がでるように焼くことです。作り方も簡単で、和食の料理教室でも人気のメニューです。フライパンで鶏肉の両面を焼いて取り出し、酒、みりん、砂糖、しょうゆを入れて煮つめたら、焼いた鶏肉を戻してソースをからめます。鶏肉が定番ですが、魚の切り身などを照り焼きにすることもあります。

海外では、TERIYAKIとしてよく知られ、スーパーマーケットで Teriyaki Sauce も売られています。

"*Teriyaki*" means grilling meat or fish with sweet soy sauce till glazed. It's an easy dish to cook and is a popular menu item in Japanese cooking classes. Grill both sides of the chicken in a frying pan, take it out, add *sake*, *mirin*, sugar and soy sauce to the pan, simmer it, then put the chicken back in and cook till glazed. This style of cooking is common for chicken, but also good for fish.

"*Teriyaki*" is well known overseas, and *teriyaki*-sauce for cooking *teriyaki* can be found in foreign supermarkets.

豚肉のしょうが焼き

[*Butaniku no Shogayaki* (Grilled Pork in Ginger)]

しょうがのきいたタレで薄切りの豚肉を焼きます。
Thinly sliced pork grilled in a ginger sauce.

薄切りの豚ロース肉に、小麦粉（または片栗粉）をふ
りかけ、フライパンで両面焼いてから、タレ（おろししょ
うが、しょうゆ、みりん、酒を混ぜたもの）を入れ、よ
くからまるまで焼きます。食欲をそそり、ごはんが進む味
つけなので、家庭料理として人気が高く、定食屋でも
「しょうが焼き定食」は、古くから愛される定番メニュー
です。

Sprinkle wheat flour (or potato starch) on thinly sliced
pork loin, grill both sides in a frying pan, add sauce (a
mixture of grated ginger, soy sauce, *mirin*, and *sake*)
and grill until glazed. This is popular as a home-
cooked dish because the flavor is so appetizing that
you can eat more rice with it. And even at diners, the
"*shogayaki* set meal" is a classic menu option that has
been loved for a long time.

和風ハンバーグ

[Japanese-style Hamburger Steak]

ハンバーグに紫蘇や大根おろしをのせ、ポン酢をかけます。
**Hamburger steak served with *shiso*, grated *daikon* and
ponzu sauce.***

ハンバーグは、ドイツのハンブルグの名物料理である肉
団子（フリカデレ）がはじまりとされています。
和風ハンバーグは、紫蘇や大根おろしをのせて、ポン
酢をかけたさっぱりとした味わいです。日本では家庭料
理として定着し、ファミリーレストランでは、デミグラス、
照り焼きなどの定番の味付けと並んで人気のメニューの1
つです。

The hamburger steak is said to have originated from
meatballs (Frikadelle), a specialty of Hamburg in
Germany.

Japanese-style hamburger steak has a refreshing taste
served with *shiso*, grated *daikon* and *ponzu* sauce. It
has become a home-cooked dish in Japan, and it is one
of the most popular menu items at family restaurants,
along with the one using standard seasonings such as
demiglace sauce and *teriyaki* sauce.

ponzu sauce: soy sauce with squeezed citrus juice seasoned with flakes
of *katsuo-bushi* (dried bonite) and kelp

居酒屋ってどんなところ？

What is an *izakaya* like?

居酒屋は、料理も酒も種類が多く、カジュアルな雰囲
気や価格で食事を楽しめる場所です。江戸時代（1603
〜 1867 年）に酒屋で酒を飲ませるようになり、酒と一
緒に酒の肴も提供するようになったのが、居酒屋の起源
といわれています。ひと昔前までは、会社員が仕事帰
りに立ち寄るイメージがありました。今はおしゃれな雰囲
気の居酒屋や、料理や酒にこだわりのあるお店も増え、
幅広い層の客が訪れるようになりました。

An *izakaya* is a place where you can enjoy meals in a
casual atmosphere and good prices, with many choices
of food and *sake*. The roots of *izakaya* are said to be
the liquor stores of the Edo period (1603-1867) that
began to serve *sake* and later side dishes with *sake*.
Until some time ago, people had the impression that an
izakaya was a place that office workers dropped into
on their way home from work. But now a wide range of
customers are attracted to them because there are more
izakayas with a fashionable atmosphere and with more
signature food and drinks.

枝豆は人気のおつまみ

Edamame is a popular appetizers

海外でも、Edamame として知られている枝豆ですが、実は熟す前の大豆を茹でたものだと知っている人は少ないようです。枝豆とよばれているのは、枝に豆がついたまま茹でたからだそうです。日本食ブームと健康ブームで海外でも知られるようになりました。アメリカではフットボール観戦時のスナックにもなっているそうです。

Edamame is also known by its Japanese name, "*edamame*," overseas, but it seems that only a few people know that it is actually soybeans that are boiled before they have ripened. It is called *edamame* (literally meaning branch beans) because the beans used to be boiled while still attached to the branches.

It has become known overseas due to the boom in both Japanese food and health.

In the United States, it is also eaten as a snack when watching football.

焼き鳥

[*Yakitori*]

一口サイズの鶏肉を竹串に刺して焼いたものです。
Grilled bite-sized chicken pieces on a bamboo skewer.

焼き鳥は、専門店や居酒屋で酒のつまみとして楽しんだり、祭りのときに出る屋台で売られたりすることが多い食べ物です。さまざまな部位があり、好みで選びます。定番の「ねぎま」は、鶏肉（もも肉、または胸肉）と長ねぎを交互に挟んだもので、味つけは甘辛いタレか塩を選びます。

You can enjoy *yakitori* as a snack at *yakitori* restaurants or
izakayas. It is often sold at stalls on festival occasions. It is
made from various parts of the chicken, and you can choose
your favorite. The standard *yakitori* is "*negima*," meaning
"between green onions." It is made by threading green onions
and chicken (thigh meat or breast meat) alternately on a
skewer and grilling them. You can choose sweetened soy sauce
or salt for seasoning.

焼き鳥の種類いろいろ

[Types of *Yakitori*]

つくね
Tsukune

ミートボールとして知られています。軟骨入りもあります。
Known as meatballs, sometimes chopped cartilage is included in the mixture as well.

もも
Thigh

ジューシーで柔らかい、鶏肉そのものを味わえる定番です。
A classic *yakitori*. Juicy and tender, and you can taste the chicken itself.

皮
Skin

パリパリに焼けた皮の食感は、おつまみとしても人気です。
The crispy texture of the grilled skin is also popular as a snack.

鉄板焼き

[*Teppan-yaki*]

肉、魚介、野菜などの食材をシェフが目の前で調理してくれます。

A chef cooks ingredients such as meat, seafood, and vegetables right in front of you.

鉄板焼きには、和牛やエビなど高価な食材を使うこと
が多く、特別な日の外食に選ばれる料理です。目の前
にある大きな鉄板で、シェフが調理するスタイルが人気
で、旅行の最終日のディナーに鉄板焼きを選ばれる海
外の方も多くいます。1960年代にアメリカに開店した
BENIHAHA という日本の鉄板焼きレストランが、ジャ
グリングなどのパフォーマンスをしながら調理すると有名
になったことから、海外で TEPPAN-YAKI の名前が
広まりました。

Teppan-yaki is the choice for dining out on special
occasions because it often involves the use of expensive
ingredients such as Japanese beef and shrimps. The
cooking style where the chef cooks on a large iron plate
in front of you is popular, and many overseas visitors
choose to have *teppan-yaki* for dinner on the last day
of their trip. Since Benihana, a Japanese *teppan-yaki*
restaurant that opened in the United States in the
1960s, became famous because the chefs cooked while
juggling and giving other performances, the name
"*teppan-yaki*" has spread the world.

炉ばた焼き

[*Robata-yaki*]

好みの食材をシェフが目の前の七輪で焼いてくれます。
A chef grills your favorite ingredients on the charcoal
brazier in front of you.

炉ばた焼きは、人気の高い外食のひとつです。炭をおこした七輪の前に座ったシェフと、さまざまな食材を取り囲むようにカウンターがつくられ、好みの食材を注文すると、シェフが目の前で焼いてくれます。焼きあがったものは、大きなかけ声とともに、オールのような長い木べらの先にのせて差し出してくれるなど、劇場のようなパフォーマンスをしてくれるお店もあります。

「炉ばた」とは、「囲炉裏（日本の昔ながらの民家にある炉）のそば」という意味の言葉です。

Robata-yaki is one of the most popular styles of dining out. A chef sits in front of a charcoal brazier and various ingredients are displayed inside a counter. When guests have ordered their favorite ingredients, the chef grills them in front of them. In some *Robata* restaurants, the chef gives a theatrical performance, such as putting the grilled food on the end of a long wooden oar and serving it to the guest with a loud shout.

Robata means "near the hearth (that is, a hearth in a traditional Japanese house)."

和牛

Wagyu beef

和牛は、"*Wagyu* Beef"として、海外の方にも知られています。肉に脂肪が霜降り状に入っていることが特徴です。牛にビールを飲ませたり、マッサージをするとおいしくなるという話もありますが、専門家によると、必ずしもそうではないとのことです。牛がリラックスする環境作りと、牧草に穀物や稲わらなどを加えて配合した良質の飼料を食べさせることが、おいしい肉の秘訣だそうです。

Wagyu is also known to foreigners as "*Wagyu* Beef." It is characterized by the fact that the meat is marbled with fat. Some say that they make cows drink beer and give them massages, but experts say that's not always the case. It is said that the secret of this delicious meat involves creating an environment where the cows can relax and feeding them with high-quality feed that is made by adding grains and rice straw to their pasture-based diet.

【ブランド和牛】 神戸牛
[Branded *wagyu*] Kobe beef

今では日本各地に品質保証されたブランド和牛があります
が、海外の方に一番有名なのは Kobe Beef です。明治
時代（1868 ～ 1912 年）に神戸に入港した外国人が食
べた、おいしい牛肉の評判が世界に広がったからです。

Nowadays, there are quality-guaranteed branded *wagyu*
beef products all over Japan, but Kobe beef is the most
famous overseas. This is because this delicious beef was
eaten by foreigners who arrived in Kobe port during
the Meiji era (1868-1912) and they spread its reputation
throughout the world.

【地鶏】 名古屋コーチン
[*Ji-dori*] Nagoya cochin

和牛同様、鶏肉も各地で有名な地鶏が育てられています。
地鶏とは、在来種の血が 50％以上であること、そしてブロ
イラーとはちがって、ふ化後 28 日以降は平飼いで飼育さ
れている鶏のことです。名古屋コーチン、鳥取の大山地鶏
などが有名です。

Like *wagyu* beef, famous *ji-dori*, local chicken is also
produced all over Japan. To be called *ji-dori*, chicken must
have a bloodline consisting of over 50% native Japanese
breeds, and unlike broilers they have to
be raised at ground level for more than
28 days. Nagoya cochin and Daisenji
ji-dori in Tottori are famous.

Part 6

発酵食品
Fermented Food

発酵食品の健康効果は、海外からも注目が集まっています。

The health effect of fermented food is attracting attention from overseas.

みそ汁

[*Miso* Soup]

日本人の健康を支える、みそを使ったスープです。
A soup using *miso* supports the health of Japanese
people.

和食の基本は「一汁三菜」（P 169 参照）といいます
が、「一汁（スープ）」は、主にみそ汁のことを指し
ます。みそ汁は、好みの具をだしで煮て、みそをとくだ
けでつくれる日常的な家庭料理です。

「みそ」は日本の伝統的な調味料です。いろいろな種
類がありますが、大豆を主な原料とし、麹菌（カビの
一種）と塩を加えることで、大豆の成分が分解、発酵
され旨み成分ができます。発酵食品は、腸内環境を
整え免疫力を高める働きがあるといわれています。

The basics of Japanese meals are called "*ichiju sansai*"
(see page 169), and the word "*ichiju* (soup)" mainly
refers to *miso* soup. *Miso* soup is a daily home-cooked
dish that can be made simply by boiling your favorite
ingredients in *dashi* stock and adding the *miso*.

"*Miso*" is a traditional Japanese seasoning. There are
various types, but soybeans are the main raw material.
By adding *koji* (a type of mold called aspergillus) and
salt, the soybean components are decomposed and
fermented to produce *umami* components. Fermented
foods are said to have the function of adjusting the
intestinal environment and boosting immunity.

みそのいろいろ

[Types of *Miso*]

赤みそ
Red *miso*

中京地区特産の赤褐色のみそ
で、辛口と甘口があります。大
豆だけを発酵させ、香り高いの
が特徴です。

A specialty of the Chukyo
region, red *miso* is reddish-
brown in color and there are
two types, a saltier one and a
sweeter one. It is produced by
fermenting only soybeans and
is known for its aroma.

白みそ
White *miso*

米麹を多く使ってつくる甘めの
みそです。京都でつくられるみ
そが有名で、雑煮にも使います。
This is a sweet *miso* made with
a lot of malted rice. The one
produced in Kyoto is famous
and used in their *ozoni* (New
Year *mochi* soup).

米みそ
Rice *miso*

日本の各地でつくられている、最も一般的なみそです。大豆と米麹が材料です。

This is the most common *miso* and is made in various parts of Japan. The ingredients are soybeans and malted rice.

麦みそ
Wheat *miso*

大豆と麦でつくられます。九州の特産品です。北関東の一部でもつくられています。

Made from soybeans and wheat, this is a specialty of the Kyushu region. It is also made in parts of the northern Kanto region.

だしのいろいろ

[Types of *Dashi*]

かつおぶし
Katsuo-bushi

ゆでて骨を取り除いたカツオを
燻し、麹菌で発酵させて旨み
を出します。木材のように固くな
るので、うすく削ります。

Boil bonito fish and remove
the bones from them, then
smoke and ferment the bonito
with *koji* mold to bring out the
flavor. When ready, *katsuo-
bushi* is hard like wood, so
shave it thinly when using it.

昆布
Kombu kelp

水につけておいた乾燥昆布を
鍋で煮だすと、まろやかなだし
がとれます。かつおぶしといっしょ
に使うことが多いです。

By boiling dried *kombu* kelp in
a pot after soaking it in water,
you can get a mellow *dashi*
stock. It is often used together
with dried bonito.

煮干し

Niboshi

カタクチイワシを煮て干したものが一般
的です。しっかりとしただしがとれるので、
そばやうどんのつゆにも使われます。

This is usually made from boiled
and dried anchovies. Often used
for *soba* and *udon* soup because
it creates a stronger flavor.

「だし」の取り方

How to take "*dashi*," the basic broth.

和食には、かつおぶしと
昆布のだしがよく使われま
す。鍋に水と昆布を入れ、
一晩つけておきます。火に
かけて煮たったら昆布を取
り出し、かつおぶしを加え
ます。煮たったら火をとめ
て濾します。近年は手軽
にだしがとれる、「だしパッ
ク」も売っています。

Dashi broth made from *katsuo-bushi* and
kombu kelp is the basic soup stock of Japanese
cuisines. Put kelp and water in a pot and let
it soak overnight. After boiling the mixture,
remove the kelp and add *katsuo-bushi*. After
it has been boiled again, turn off the heat and
strain the soup to remove the *katsuo-bushi*.
In recent years, it has become possible to
purchase "*dashi* packs" that make it easy to
make *dashi* stock.

薬味

Yakumi condiments

薬味は、くさみを消したり、味を際立たせたり、彩りを加えたりします。消化を助け、血行促進するなど、体によいとされる働きもあります。
Yakumi are added to eliminate odors, to accentuate flavor, and add color to food. They also have medicinal efficacy such as helping digestion and promoting blood circulation.

しょうが
Ginger

熱帯アジア原産で、奈良時代（710 ～ 784）に中国から日本に伝わりました。さわやかな辛味は、魚料理のくさみ消しに使われます。体を温める効果もあります。
It is native to tropical Asia and was introduced from China to Japan during the Nara period (710-784). The refreshing pungent taste is used to remove the odors of fish dishes. It also has the effect of warming the body.

紫蘇
Shiso

紫蘇はミントの親戚で、青紫蘇と赤紫蘇があります。青紫蘇は刺身に添えられます。赤紫蘇は梅干しの色付けに使います。
Shiso belongs to the same family as mint, and there are green *shiso* and red *shiso*. The green one is served with *sashimi*. The red one is used to color pickled plums.

大根おろしと紅葉おろし
Grated *Daikon* radish & *Momiji-oroshi*

すりおろした大根には、消化を助ける酵素が含まれるので
揚げ物に添えられます。ピリッとする辛味には食中毒防止の
殺菌作用もあります。赤唐辛子を一緒にすりおろしたものは、
その赤い色から紅葉おろしとよばれます。

Grated *daikon* radish is often added to fried food because
it contains enzymes that help digestion. The spicy
pungent taste also has a bactericidal action to prevent
food poisoning. When *daikon* and red pepper are grated
together, it is called *momiji-oroshi* (grated maple leaf)
because of its red color.

刻みねぎ
Chopped green onions

刻んだねぎは、みそ汁やそばやうどんなどに入れます。身体
を温め、血行を良くする効果があるといわれます。

Chopped green onions are added to *miso* soup, *soba*
noodles, and *udon* noodles. It is said to have the effect of
warming the body and improving blood circulation.

納豆

[*Natto*]

ゆでた大豆を納豆菌で発酵させたネバネバ食品です。

**A sticky food made by fermenting boiled soybeans with
natto bacteria.**

納豆菌は枯れ草の中（とくに稲わら）の中に多く生息
している菌で、たんぱく質を分解して、旨み成分である
アミノ酸をつくりだしてくれます。

納豆には独特のにおいと糸を引くという特徴があります
が、慣れるとやみつきになるおいしさです。しょうゆ、か
らし、刻みねぎを加えて混ぜ、ごはんにのせて食べる
のが一般的です。健康的な日本の朝食に欠かせない
一品ですが、海外の方がはじめて見ると、チャレンジ
に勇気が必要な食べ物のようです。

Natto bacteria inhabits in dry grass (especially rice
straw), and decompose proteins to produce amino
acids, the source of *umami*.

Natto has a unique smell and stickiness. However,
once you get used to it, it is so delicious that it becomes
addictive. It is common to eat it by adding and mixing
with soy sauce, mustard, and chopped green onions,
then putting the mixture on rice. It is an indispensable
dish for a healthy Japanese breakfast, but it seems to
be a challenge for foreigners when trying it for the first
time.

梅干し

[*Umeboshi*]

塩辛くて酸っぱい、梅の実の漬け物です。
Salty and sour pickled plum.

日本の伝統的な漬け物です。甘くなる前の黄色い梅を、塩と
赤紫蘇に漬けてつくります。消化不良を解消して、食中毒防
止効果があるといわれ、弁当やおにぎりにもよく使われます。
海外の方は、甘いスモモだと思って食べて驚く方が多いです。
Umeboshi is a traditional Japanese pickle. It is made by
soaking yellow plums before they become sweet in salt and
red perilla. It is said to have a positive effect on indigestion
and to be able to prevent food poisoning. So, it is often used
for box lunches and rice balls. Many foreigners are surprised
when they eat it because they think it is a sweet plum.

ぬか漬け

[*Nukazuke* (Pickles in Rice-bran Mash)]

発酵させた米ぬかで野菜を漬け込む、伝統的な漬け物です。

Traditional pickled vegetables in fermented rice bran.

米ぬかを発酵させてつくる「ぬか床」を壺などに入れて野菜を漬け込み、毎日かき混ぜるなど手間をかけてつくられます。最近では、簡単に作れ、冷蔵庫に入れておけるセットも売られています。植物性乳酸菌が豊富で健康効果が注目されています。

The "*nukadoko* (pickle bed)," which is made by fermenting rice bran, is put in a jar, to which vegetables are added. You have to stir the *nukadoko* every day to expose it to oxygen. Recently, it has become possible to purchase a "*nukadoko*" set that can be easily made and stored in the refrigerator.

This type of pickling is attracting attention for the health benefits of its rich plant-derived lactic acid bacteria.

漬け物いろいろ

[Types of Pickles]

たくあん漬け
Takuan-zuke

大根を麹、塩、砂糖、唐辛子などで漬け込んだ人気の漬け物です。たくあんの黄色は、大根の辛味成分が発酵した色です。A popular pickle made by pickling *daikon* with rice bran, salt, sugar, and pepper. Its yellow color is created when the pungent component of *daikon* is fermented.

高菜漬け
Takana-zuke

アブラナ科の青菜である高菜を塩漬けにし、乳酸発酵させたものです。高菜漬けを刻んでごはんにまぜた高菜飯は、九州の名物です。It is made by salting and fermenting *takana* (leaf mustard) with lactic acid. *Takana* is a green vegetable of the Brassicaceae family. *Takana-meshi*, rice mixed with chopped *takana-zuke,* is a specialty of Kyushu.

らっきょう漬け
Rakkyo-zuke (Pickled scallions)

らっきょうはネギ科の植物で、その白い地下茎の部分を甘酢で漬けます。カレーライスに添えるのが定番です。

Rakkyo is a plant of the allioideae family, and its white rhizome is pickled in sweet vinegar. It is the standard condiment for curry rice.

奈良漬け
Nara-zuke

瓜を酒粕で漬け込んだ粕漬けです。わずかなアルコール分があります。うなぎのかば焼きと一緒に食べる習慣があります。

It is made by pickling melon with *sake* lees. Note that a small amount of alcohol remains. It is customarily eaten with eel *kabayaki*.

ご当地グルメ

Local gourmet food

日本の各地には海の幸や山の幸、そして珍しい食材を使ったご当地グルメがあります。

In various parts of Japan, there are local gourmet foods made from seafood, mountain food, and rare ingredients.

宇都宮の餃子

Ustunomiya *gyoza*

餃子の本場中国では、厚い皮の水餃子が主流なのに対し、日本では薄い皮の焼き餃子が人気です。日本流の餃子の発祥地とされる栃木県の宇都宮駅前には、たくさんの餃子専門店が立ち並び、餃子の銅像が建っています。

In China, the home of *gyoza* dumplings, thick-skinned boiled ones are the conventional type, while in Japan, thin-skinned grilled ones are popular. Many *gyoza* specialty restaurants are lined up in front of Utsunomiya Station in Tochigi Prefecture, which is said to be the birthplace of Japanese-style *gyoza*, and there is also a bronze statue of some *gyoza*.

湘南のしらす丼
Shonan *shirasu-don*

しらすは片口イワシの幼魚です。さっと茹でてごはんにのせたしらす丼は、神奈川県の湘南地区の名物です。時期によりますが、生しらす丼を提供する店もあります。

Shirasu is a young sardine, and *shirasu-don*, a bowl of rice topped with boiled *shirasu*, is a specialty of the Shonan area of Kanagawa prefecture. Depending on the season, some restaurants offer a raw *shirasu-don*.

沖縄のソーキそば
Okinawa *soki-soba*

ソーキそばは、そば粉でなく小麦粉でつくられた平らな麺を使います。スープはかつおと豚骨ベースのものが多く、人気のあるトッピングはソーキと呼ばれる豚のスペアリブをしょうゆと黒砂糖で煮込んだものです。

Soki-soba are flat noodles made from wheat flour instead of buckwheat flour. Most soups are based on dried bonito and pork bones, and a popular topping is pork spareribs called *soki* stewed in soy sauce and brown sugar.

Part 7

コース／定食
Course / Set Meal

日本のコース料理は、季節の食材を使った料理が味わえます。

A Japanese course menu is a meal made with seasonal ingredients.

会席料理

[*Kaiseki* Cuisine]

酒宴を楽しむための和食の上等なコース料理です。
A high-class Japanese course meal to enjoy banquet style.

会席料理は、酒宴を楽しむためのコース料理です。一般的な献立では、前菜、吸い物、刺身、焼き物、煮物、揚げ物、蒸し物、酢の物などが順番に運ばれ、最後にご飯とみそ汁、香の物、水菓子が出されます。食前酒が出されるときもあります。

※料理の数や順番はお店によって変わることもあります。

Kaiseki cuisine is a course meal to enjoy banquet style. In a typical menu, appetizers, soup, *sashimi*, grilled dishes, simmered dishes, deep-fried dishes, steamed dishes, and vinegared dishes are delivered in order, and finally rice and *miso* soup, pickles, and fruits are served. Some restaurants add an aperitif.

*The number of dishes and the order of serving may differ depnding on restaurants.

❶食前酒 aperitif ❷前菜 appetizers ❸吸い物 soup ❹刺身 *sashimi* ❺焼き物 grilled dishes ❻煮物 simmered dishes ❼揚げ物 deep-fried dishes ❽蒸し物 steamed dishes ❾酢の物 vinegared dishes ❿ごはん rice ⓫止め椀（赤だし）last soup （red *miso* soup）⓬香の物 pickles ⓭水菓子 fruits

懐石料理

[*Kaiseki Ryori*]

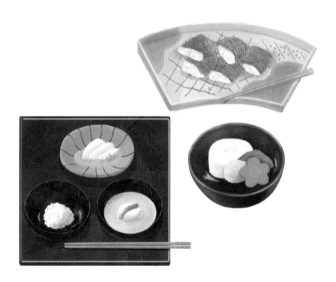

もともとはお茶の席で出される簡単な食事の意味でした。
Originally a simple meal served at the tea ceremony.

「懐石料理」と「会席料理」は、どちらもコース料理で、
読み方（音）は同じですが、違う漢字で表し、内容
もかなり違います。

「懐石」は、禅僧が修行中に寒さと空腹を忘れるため
に、懐に温めた石を抱えたという逸話に由来して「飢え
をしのぐ程度の粗末な食事」という意味があります。お
茶の席でされる濃いお茶を楽しむ前に、おなかを整える
ための一汁三菜の料理です。

There are two types of "*kaiseki ryori.*" Both are course
meals and have the same reading (sound), but they are
expressed in different *kanji* and the contents are quite
different.

In this case, "*kaiseki*" means "a poor meal enough to
survive hunger" from the anecdote that a *Zen* priest
held a warm stone in his robe to forget the cold and
hunger during his training. It consists of soup, rice and
three dishes to prepare your stomach before enjoying
the strong tea served at the tea ceremony.

精進料理

[*Shojin Ryori*]

禅寺での食事が発展した和のベジタリアンのお膳です。
A Japanese vegetarian meal developed at *Zen* temples.

日本に仏教が伝来してからはじまった料理です。仏教の戒律である殺生や煩悩への刺激をさけるため、魚や肉、玉ねぎなどの臭いの強い食材を使いません。命をいただく感謝をこめて材料のすべてを使い切ることを基本とし、禅僧が修行の一環として寺で調理をします。精進料理に出される「けんちん汁」は、野菜をごま油で炒めて、昆布やシイタケのだしでつくります。鎌倉の禅寺「建長寺」の修行僧がつくっていたことからこの名前がついたそうです。

This style of meal began after Buddhism was introduced to Japan. It does not include fish, meat or strong-smelling ingredients such as onions to avoid the killing of living beings and the stimulating of worldly desires in line with the Buddhist commandments. *Zen* priests cook at the temple as part of their training, and use up everything in gratitude for the ingredients' existence.

The dish "*kenchin-jiru*" served in this course meal is made by stir-frying vegetables in sesame oil and simmering them in *dashi* broth flavored by kelp and *shiitake* mushrooms. It is said that this name was given to the dish because it was invented by a monk of the *Zen* temple "*Kenchoji*" in Kamakura.

定食

[*Teishoku* (Set Meal)]

食堂や料理屋で食べる、組み合わせが決められたセット料理です。

A set meal of a fixed combination of dishes that you can eat at a cafeteria or restaurant.

一般的には、メインのおかず、みそ汁、ごはん、漬け物がセットになっています。メインの料理はバリエーションが豊かで、てんぷら定食、刺身定食など、メインの料理の名前でよびます。手ごろな値段で食べられるので、学生や会社員の昼食に最適です。

Generally, *teishoku* includes a main dish, *miso* soup, rice, and pickles. Main dishes have a wide variety, and the set meal is called by the name of the main dish, such as *tempura* set meal or *sashimi* set meal. Set meals are reasonably priced and make an ideal lunch for students and office workers.

日本の朝ごはん

Japanese breakfast

最近は、日本人でも朝はパンとコーヒーという人も多くいますが、ごはん、みそ汁、焼き魚をメインに、漬け物、焼き海苔、納豆などを合わせるのが、日本の伝統的な朝ごはんです。栄養価が高いことが特徴です。

ところで、和食の基本は「一汁三菜」といいます。ごはん、汁物、漬け物に、なます、焼き物、煮物の三品を加えた組み合わせのことです。複数のおかずを、ひとつのお膳にのせて楽しめるのも和食の特徴です。

Recently, many Japanese people have started to prefer bread and coffee in the morning, but a traditional Japanese breakfast mainly consists of rice, *miso* soup and grilled fish together with a choice of pickles, grilled *nori* kelp, and *natto*. It is known for its high nutritional value.

By the way, the basic Japanese meal is based on the concept of "*Ichiju Sansai*." It consists of rice, soup, pickles, vinegared food, grilled food, and simmered food. One of the characteristics of Japanese cuisine is that you can enjoy multiple side dishes served on a tray.

Part 8

和菓子／果物
Japanese Cake / Fruit

小豆を甘く煮る習慣がないので、あんこは多くの海外の方にとって新しい味わいです。

It is not common to cook red beans sweetly outside of Japan. So, for most foreigners eating *anko* is a new experience.

172/
ねりきり
Neri-kiri

174/
だんご
Dango (Dumpling)

175/
ぼたもち・おはぎ
Botamochi · Ohagi

176/
あんみつ
Anmitsu

177/
どら焼き
Dorayaki (Sweet Bean Gongs)

178/
かき氷
Shaved Ice

180/
せんべい
Senbei

184/
柿
Kaki

185/
メロン
Melon

186/
みかん
Mikan

187/
りんご
Apple

ねりきり

[*Neri-kiri*]

季節を感じることができるデザートの芸術品です。
This Japanese confectionery is a work of art that gives
you a sense of the seasons.

ねりきりは、上生菓子ともいわれます。白大豆やインゲ
ン豆に砂糖を加えてつくった白あんを、木べらや木型な
どを使って季節の花など美しい形に整えたお菓子です。
格式が高く、お祝いの席やお客様へのおもてなしとして
用いられるほかに、お茶会で抹茶に合わせるお菓子と
しても使われます。「黒文字（くろもじ）」とよばれるお
菓子専用の楊枝を使って食べます。

Neri-kiri is also called *jo-namagashi*. White bean paste
made by adding sugar to white soybeans and white
kidney beans is used to make beautiful shapes such as
seasonal flowers using wooden spatula and wooden
molds.

It is highly prestigious and is used not only for
celebrations and entertaining guests, but also as sweets
served with *matcha* at tea ceremonies. Eat using a
special toothpick for sweets called a "*kuromoji*."

だんご

[*Dango* (Dumpling)]

粉を水でこねて丸めて茹でたり蒸したりして竹串に刺したものです。

The powder is kneaded with water, rolled, boiled or steamed, and put on a bamboo skewer.

上新粉（米の粉）や白玉粉でつくります。竹串に刺さっている姿がかわいらしく、人気の理由です。「みたらし」という、しょうゆ、砂糖、片栗粉で作った甘辛のタレをかけたり、あんこをのせて食べます。粉とともに抹茶を入れた茶団子も人気です。

It is made from powder called *joshinko* (rice flour) or *shiratamako*. It is popular because of the cute shape put on a bamboo skewer. The one served with sweet soy sauce made from soy sauce, sugar, and potato starch is called "*mitarashi*" and there is also the one with *anko* (sweet red bean paste). Tea dumplings using the powder mixed with *matcha* are also popular.

ぼたもち・おはぎ

[*Botamochi* and *Ohagi*]

蒸したもち米をつぶして丸め、あんこをまぶしたものです。
Confectionery made by crushing steamed glutinous
rice, rolling it, and covering it with *anko* (red bean
paste).

ぼたもちというのは、春に咲く牡丹の花から名づけられました。
形は丸く、こしあんを使います。一方、おはぎは、秋に咲く萩
の花から名づけられたものです。形は米俵型で粒あんが使わ
れます。どちらも、お彼岸に先祖の霊を慰め、邪気を払うため
につくられた伝統的なお菓子です。

Botamochi is named after the peony flowers that bloom in the
spring. It has a round shape and is covered in smooth red bean
paste. On the other hand, *ohagi* is named after the *hagi* flower
that blooms in the autumn, and is shaped like an oval rice bag
coated in chunky red bean paste. Both are traditional sweets
made during the equinoctial week to comfort ancestral spirits
and ward off evil spirits.

あんみつ

[*Anmitsu*]

ノーカロリーの寒天に、あんこをのせたスイーツです。
**A dessert of calorie-free agar jelly served with *anko* on
top.**

ダイス型に切った寒天に、ゆでた赤えんどう、フルーツ、求肥、
あんこをのせ、黒蜜をかけて食べます。求肥は白玉粉を蒸し、
砂糖を加えて固めたものです。あんこをのせないものは、「蜜豆」
といいます。寒天は、植物性繊維がたっぷりの健康食品です。
Boiled red peas, fruits, *gyuhi*, and red bean paste are placed
on agar jelly cut into small cubes served with dark molasses.
Gyuhi is made by steaming *shiratamako* and adding sugar to
harden it. Those without red bean paste on them are called
"*mitsumame*." Agar is a healthy food with plenty of vegetable
fiber.

どら焼き

[*Dorayaki* (Sweet Bean Gongs)]

小さな 2 枚のパンケーキに、あんこをはさんだ人気のおやつです。

A popular snack of sweet red bean paste sandwiched between two small pancakes.

打楽器の「どら」に形が似ているので、どら焼きと名付けられたといわれています。関西では、奈良県の三笠山にちなんで「三笠」とよぶ地域もあります。海外の方は、甘く調理した豆になじみがない方が多いのですが、あんこは和スイーツの定番です。

This dessert is said to have been named *dorayaki* because it resembles the "*dora* (gong)" a percussion instrument. In the Kansai region, it is called "*mikasa*" after Mt. Mikasa in Nara Prefecture. Many foreigners are unfamiliar with sweetly cooked beans, but *anko* is a basic component of Japanese desserts.

かき氷

[Shaved Ice]

削って雪状にした氷に、シロップなどをかけたものです。
Shaved snow-like ice served with syrup on top.

夏の定番デザートです。バリエーション豊かで、ピンクは「イチゴ」、緑は「メロン」、黄色は「レモン」など、鮮やかな色と香りをつけたシロップを使うのが一般的です。最近では本物のイチゴをつぶしたソースを使う高級なかき氷店も人気です。
Shaved ice is a classic summer dessert. There are many variations, and it is common to use syrup with bright colors and scents, such as pink for "strawberry," green for "melon," and yellow for "lemon." Recently, high-class shaved ice shops that use the sauce of crushed real strawberries have also become popular.

かき氷の種類いろいろ

[Types of Shaved Ice]

イチゴみるく
Strawberry milk

イチゴシロップの上に甘い練乳
をかけたかき氷です。練乳は
人気のトッピングで、ほかのシ
ロップとの組み合わせもありま
す。

Shaved ice with sweet
condensed milk on top of
strawberry syrup. Condensed
milk is a popular topping and
can be combined with other
syrups.

宇治金時
Uji kintoki

宇治はお茶の名産地の名前で
す。抹茶シロップの上に粒あん
をのせます。白玉やアイスクリー
ムをのせることが多いです。
Uji is the name of a famous
tea producing area. The red
bean paste is put on top of
the *matcha* syrup. It is also
often served with additional
toppings such as rice-flour
dumplings or ice cream.

179

せんべい

[Senbei]

Rice cracker として、海外でも知られています。
Known abroad as rice crackers.

手軽なおやつの定番です。うるち米（ごはんとして食べる米）を蒸してつぶし、平たく丸く伸ばしてから、乾かしたものを焼いたものです。しょうゆや塩で味つけし、ごま入りの（またはごまをふる）もの、海苔を巻くものもあります。

うるち米ではなく、もち米からつくるものは「おかき」とよびます。せんべいによく似ていますが、食感はせんべいの方が硬いという特徴があります。

Senbei is a typical easy snack. *Uruchi* rice (ordinary rice) is steamed, squashed, flattened, shaped into rounds, dried and grilled. Seasoned with soy sauce or salt, some of them include sesame seeds or are wrapped in *nori*.

Those made from *mochi* (glutinous) rice instead of *uruchi* rice are called "*okaki*." They look similar, but *senbei* is harder than *okaki*.

日本のお茶について

Japanese tea

日本茶は、健康食としての和食ブームに伴って海外でも急速に人気が高まっています。日本茶に多く含まれる成分のカテキンはポリフェノールの一種で、抗酸化作用、抗がん効果があるとされています。とくに抹茶はお茶の葉そのものを飲用するため、ビタミンCなどお茶の栄養素をしっかり取り入れることができます。

Japanese tea is rapidly gaining popularity overseas with the boom in Japanese food as a health food. Catechin, a component of Japanese tea, is a type of polyphenol and is said to have antioxidant and anti-cancer effects. And with *matcha* especially, you can take in all the tea nutrients including such as vitamin C because you drink the whole tea leaves.

お茶の種類
Types of tea

煎茶 *Sencha*

日常的によく飲まれる緑茶。
収穫した茶の葉を蒸らし、
乾燥後、もんで茶葉を柔ら
かくする。

Green tea that is often
drunk in daily life. Steam
the harvested tea leaves,
dry them, and rub them to
soften the tea leaves.

玉露 *Gyokuro*

上質な緑茶。茶葉の収穫前に
2週間以上覆いをかけて栽培す
ることで、カテキンがテアニンとい
う旨みに変わる。

Gyokuro is a high quality
green tea. The tea is grown by
covering the tree for more than
two weeks before harvesting,
and in this way the catechin
changes to theanine which
creates *umami*.

抹茶 *Matcha*

伝統的な茶会でよく飲まれる。
茶葉の収穫前に覆いをかけて
育てたものを蒸らし、乾燥した
後に、石臼などで粉末にしたも
の。

Matcha is often drunk at
traditional tea ceremonies.
Tea leaves grown by covering
the tree before harvesting
are steamed, dried, and then
powdered with a stone mill.

ほうじ茶 *Hojicha*

日常的によく飲まれる。茶の葉を
キツネ色になるまで強火で煎って
香ばしくしたもので、カフェインも
少ない。

Hojicha is often drunk in daily
life.The tea leaves are roasted
over a high heat until they
turn golden brown to make
them fragrant and contain less
caffeine.

柿

[*Kaki*]

日本から欧米に紹介された果物です。
A fruit introduced from Japan to Europe and the United States.

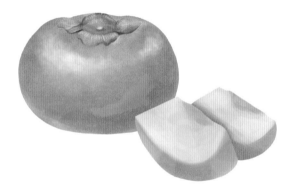

栄養価が高く、抗酸化作用のあるカテキンを含み、ひとつで一日に必要なビタミン C を取ることができるスーパーフルーツです。日本から紹介された果物なので、ヨーロッパやアメリカでもKAKIと日本名で知られています。

Kaki is a super fruit that is nutritious and contains catechins, which have antioxidant properties, and the necessary amount of vitamin C for one day. Since it is a fruit introduced from Japan, it is known as *kaki* in Europe and the United States.

メロン

[Melon]

デパチカで売られる高価なメロンに海外の方は驚きます。
Foreign visitors are surprised to see expensive melons
sold in *depachika* (grocery shops in department stores).

海外では Cantaloupe の名前で同じ種類のメロンが廉価で
売られており、その価格差に興味を持たれます。日本の高価な
メロンは、おいしさにこだわり、一本の茎から一個しか収穫し
ないなど、大事に温室栽培することでブランド化したのです。
The same type of melon is sold overseas at a low price under
the name of cantaloupe, so foreign visitors are surprised about
the price difference. Japan's expensive melons are branded by
carefully cultivating them in the greenhouse, harvesting only
one from each stem, and focusing on the deliciousness.

みかん

[*Mikan*]

温州みかんは、皮が柔らかくて手で簡単にむけます。
Unshu mikan has a soft skin and can be easily peeled by
hand.

柑橘類は世界中で栽培されていますが、日本の温州みかん
は、海外では、まだ一般的ではありません。最近は日本から
の輸出も増加しており、テレビを見ながら皮をむけるので TV
Orange というニックネームもあります。
Citrus fruits are cultivated all over the world, but Japanese
unshu mikan is not yet common overseas. Recently, exports
from Japan have been increasing, and these fruits are
sometimes called by the nickname, TV Orange, because you
can peel off their skin while watching TV.

りんご

[Apple]

日本のりんごの味と、見た目の良さは海外でも有名です。
Japanese apples are known overseas for their taste and
good appearance.

甘さと酸味のバランスがよい 「ふじ」 という品種が、 海外の方
に人気があり、 台湾、 香港などへの輸出が増えています。 欧
米では、そのままランチに持参できる小さめのサイズが多いので、
日本のりんごの大きさと形が整っていることに驚きます。
A variety called "*Fuji*," which has a good balance of sweetness
and sourness, is popular with foreigners, and the exports to
Taiwan, Hong Kong, etc. are increasing. In Europe and the
United States, most apples are small and easy to include in a
packed lunch, so the people there are surprised to find that
Japanese apples are large and uniform in shape.

人気の観光スポット「デパチカ」

Popular tourist spots "*Depachika*"

最近では海外の方の 「日本で行ってみたいところ」 の リストに "*Depachika*" が入るようになるほど、 日本の デパートの地下食品売り場が注目を浴びています。 売 り場面積の広さ、 品物の種類の多さ、 陳列の美し さは、 他に類を見ないそうで、 売り場に入った瞬間に 「Overwhelming! （すごい！）」 と歓声があがり、 長 い時間をかけて見学や試食を楽しまれる海外の方が多 くいます。

In recent years, "*depachika*," the underground food department of Japanese department stores has gained so much attention that *depachika* has been added to the list of places that foreign visitors want to visit in Japan. They say that the large area of the sales floor, the variety of items, and the beauty of the displays are unparalleled, and the moment they enter the sales floor, they exclaim that it is "Overwhelming!," and spend a long time there looking at and tasting the foods.

総菜や鮮魚コーナー
Delicatessen and fresh fish corner

種類豊富な総菜や、魚河岸のような鮮魚のコーナーが人気。
A wide variety of delicatessen items and the fresh fish
corner are reminiscent of the fish market are popular.

フルーツやスイーツコーナー
Fruits and sweets corner

高級フルーツや、華やかなスイーツは注目の的。
High-end fruits and gorgeous sweets are the focus of
attention.

おわりに

私は海外からのお客様に日本をご案内する全国通訳案内士という仕事をしています。日本の伝統的な寺社や景勝地をご案内することが多いのですが、近年お客様の「日本でしたいこと」のリストで急浮上しているのが「本物の和食を食べたい」ということです。

今や伝統的な和食だけでなく、ラーメンやうどんやオムライスなどの人気も高まり、これらを日本のお店で食べてみたいと希望する海外の方が増えているのです。また、SNSやブログなどを通じ、日本人でも知らないような店の情報を事前に調べてくる方もいらっしゃいます。

本書では、伝統的な和食はもちろん、家庭料理や、居酒屋の人気メニュー、そして和食にまつわるコラムなども幅広く掲載しました。海外からのお客様に「現在の和食」を知っていただく一助になれば幸いです。

Afterword

I work as a national certified interpreter-guide to guide customers from overseas all over Japan. I often take them to traditional Japanese temples and shrines and scenic spots, but in recent years what has suddenly appeared on the customers' "wish list" of things to do in Japan is "to eat real Japanese food." Today, not only traditional Japanese food but also *ramen* and *udon* noodles and *omurice* are becoming popular, so more people are interested in visiting Japan to try to eat them. Some people even search SNS and blogs in advance for information on some specialty restaurants and infomation that Japanese people don't know about.

Therefore, this book introduces not only traditional Japanese food, but also home-cooked food and popular items on *izakaya* menus as well as columns on *Washoku*. I hope that this book will help visitors from overseas to know about "current Japanese food."

著者　松本美江（MATSUMOTO Yoshie）

同志社大学文学部英文学科卒業。米国コロラド大学にて言語学と英語教授法で修士号を取得。通訳案内業試験に合格後、通訳ガイドとして活動。30年以上のキャリアを持ち、世界各国からの観光客数万人のガイドを担当。

協同組合全日本通訳案内士連盟（JFG）理事長として、全国通訳案内士試験合格者向けの研修も担当している。著書に『英語でガイドする日本』（ジャパンタイムズ出版）、『英語で紹介する日本』（ナツメ社）、『英語で日本紹介ハンドブック』（アルク）などがある。

本書に関するお問い合わせは、書名・発行日・該当ページを明記の上、下記のいずれかの方法にてお送りください。電話でのお問い合わせはお受けしておりません。
・ナツメ社 web サイトの問い合わせフォーム
　https://www.natsume.co.jp/contact
・FAX（03-3291-1305）
・郵送（下記、ナツメ出版企画株式会社宛て）
　なお、回答までに日にちをいただく場合があります。正誤のお問い合わせ以外の書籍内容に関する解説・個別の相談は行っておりません。あらかじめご了承ください。

WASHOKU
Japanese Traditional Food and Food Culture

ナツメ社Webサイト
https://www.natsume.co.jp
書籍の最新情報（正誤情報を含む）は
ナツメ社Webサイトをご覧ください。

2021年7月9日　初版発行
2023年10月10日　第2刷発行

著　者	松本美江	©Matsumoto Yoshie,2021
発行者	田村正隆	

発行所　株式会社ナツメ社
　　　　〒101-0051 東京都千代田区神田神保町1-52 ナツメ社ビル1F
　　　　TEL 03-3291-1257（代表）　FAX 03-3291-5761
　　　　振替 00130-1-58661
制　作　ナツメ出版企画株式会社
　　　　〒101-0051 東京都千代田区神田神保町1-52 ナツメ社ビル3F
　　　　TEL 03-3295-3921（代表）
印刷所　ラン印刷社

ISBN978-4-8163-7044-1　　　　　　　　　　　　　　　　Printed in Japan